Brackenbury Primary School
Dalling Road
Hammersmith
London, W6 0BA

icanhascheezburger?

# HAS ZBURGER?

**A LOLcat Colleckshun**

**Professor Happycat**
**& icanhascheezburger.com**

HODDER &
STOUGHTON

First published in Great Britain in 2008 by Hodder & Stoughton
An Hachette Livre UK company

4

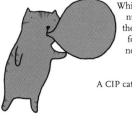

While the author has made every effort to provide accurate telephone
numbers and internet addresses at the time of publication, neither
the publisher nor the author assumes any responsibility for errors, or
for changes that occur after publication. Further, the publisher does
not have any control over and does not assume any responsibility for
author or third party websites or their content.

A CIP catalogue record for this title is available from the British Library

ISBN 978 0340 977576

Set in **IMPACT!!1!**
Designed bai Ben Gibson
Illustrations bai Lianne Uesato and Kenta Nemoto

Printed and bound in Italy by Lego

Hodder & Stoughton policy is to use papers that are natural, renewable and recyclable products
and made from wood grown in sustainable forests. The logging and manufacturing processes
are expected to conform to the environmental regulations of the country of origin.

Hodder & Stoughton Ltd
338 Euston Road
London NW1 3BH
www.hodder.co.uk

No kittehs were harmd in the making of dis book.

OH HAI

I BUFFED UR FLOOR

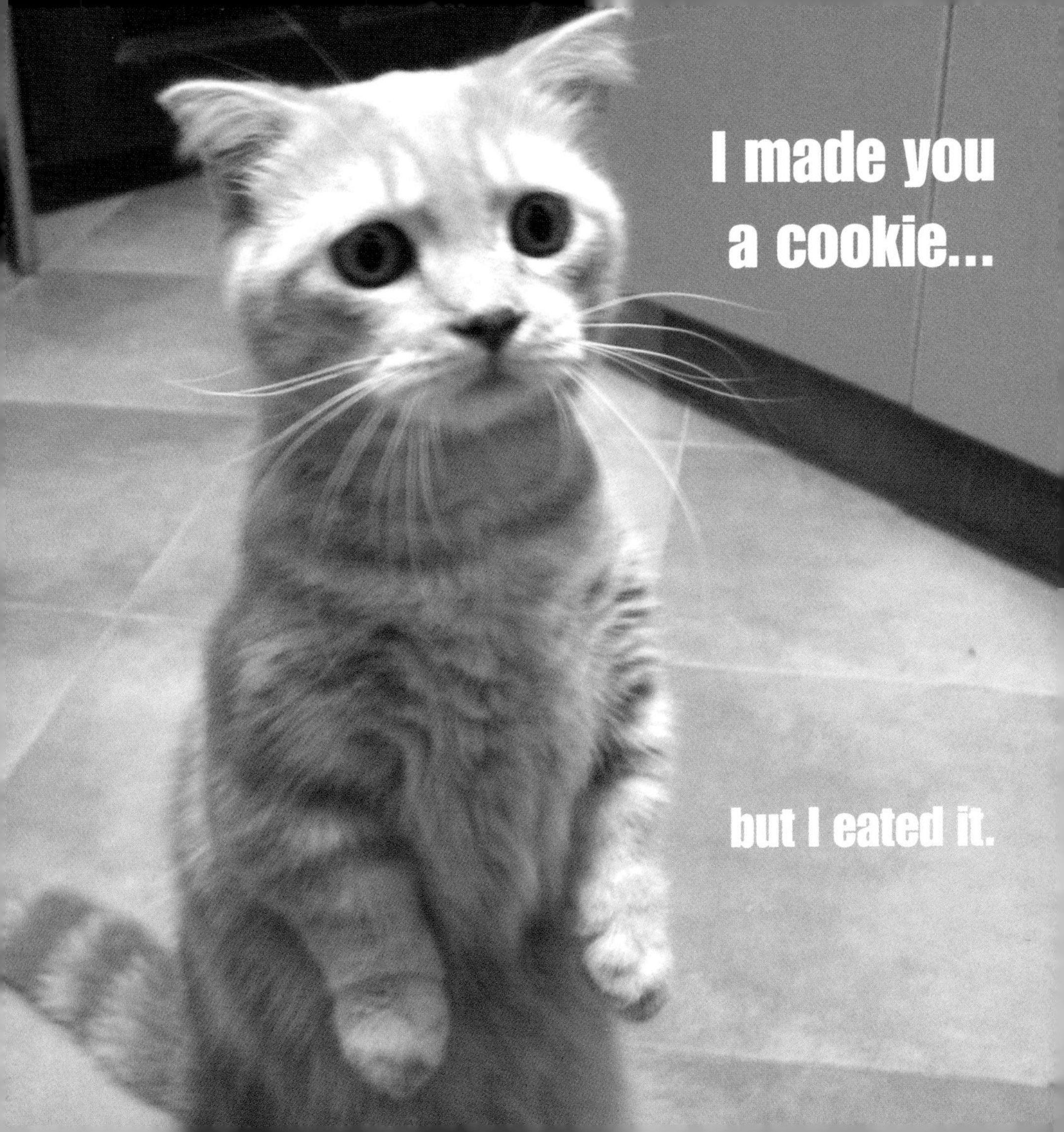
I made you
a cookie...
but I eated it.

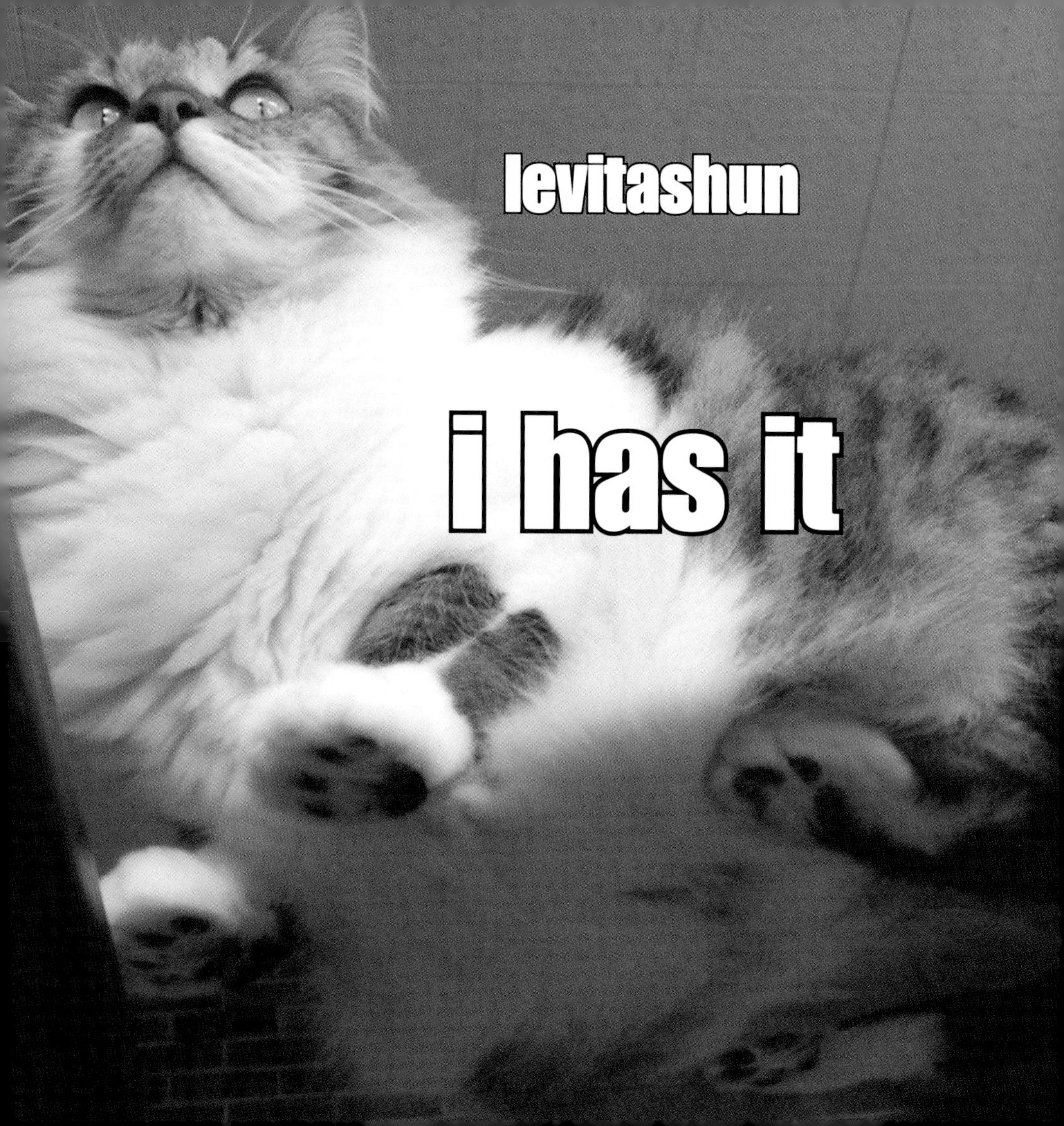
levitashun
i has it

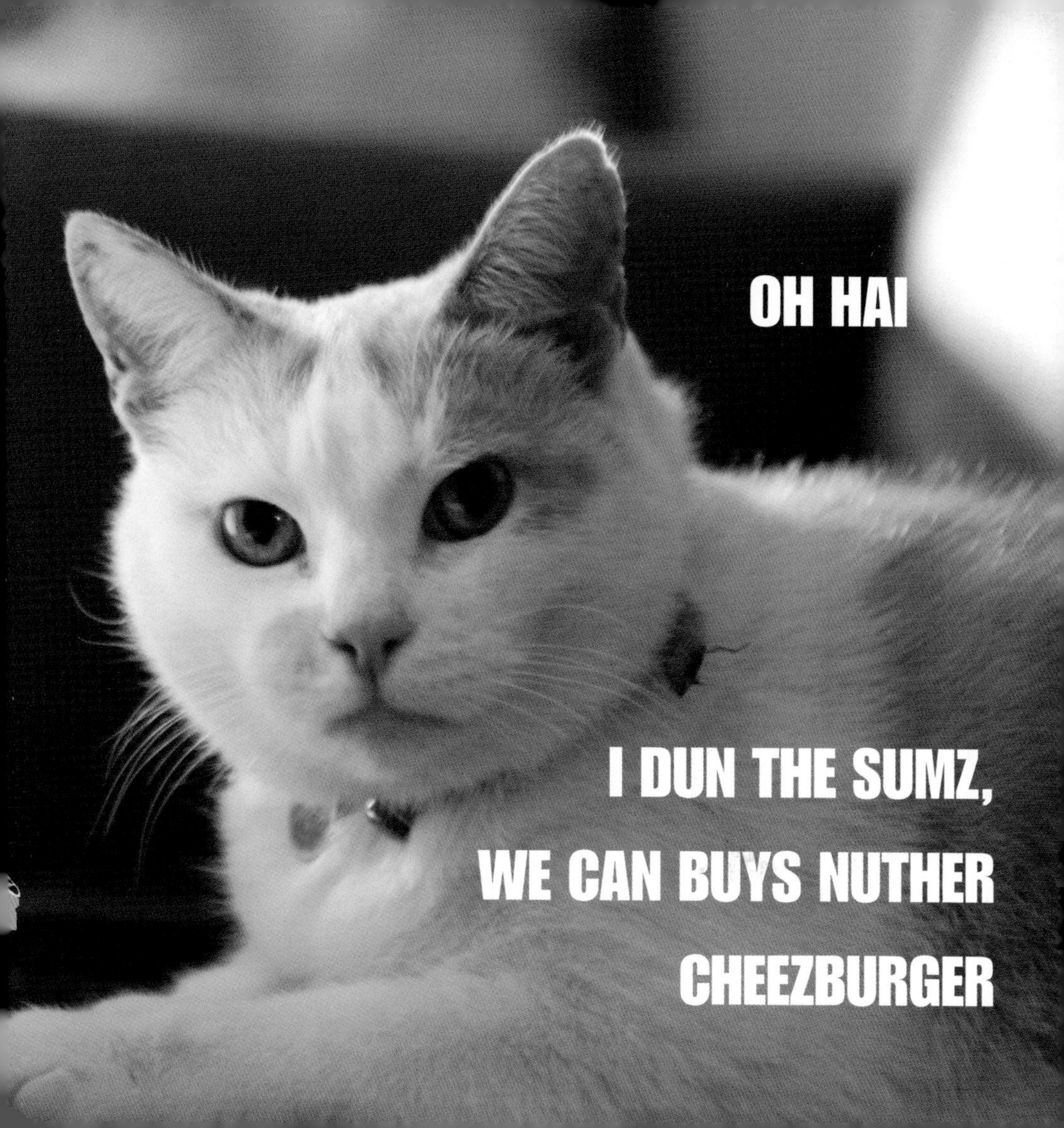
OH HAI
I DUN THE SUMZ,
WE CAN BUYS NUTHER
CHEEZBURGER

mai preshussss

# MONORAIL CAT

# MONORAIL CAT
ideel kitteh methud of travelng,
tho never on time and offen out
of servis

turn the gravity back on, ok ha!?

gah!!!

is full of starz!!!

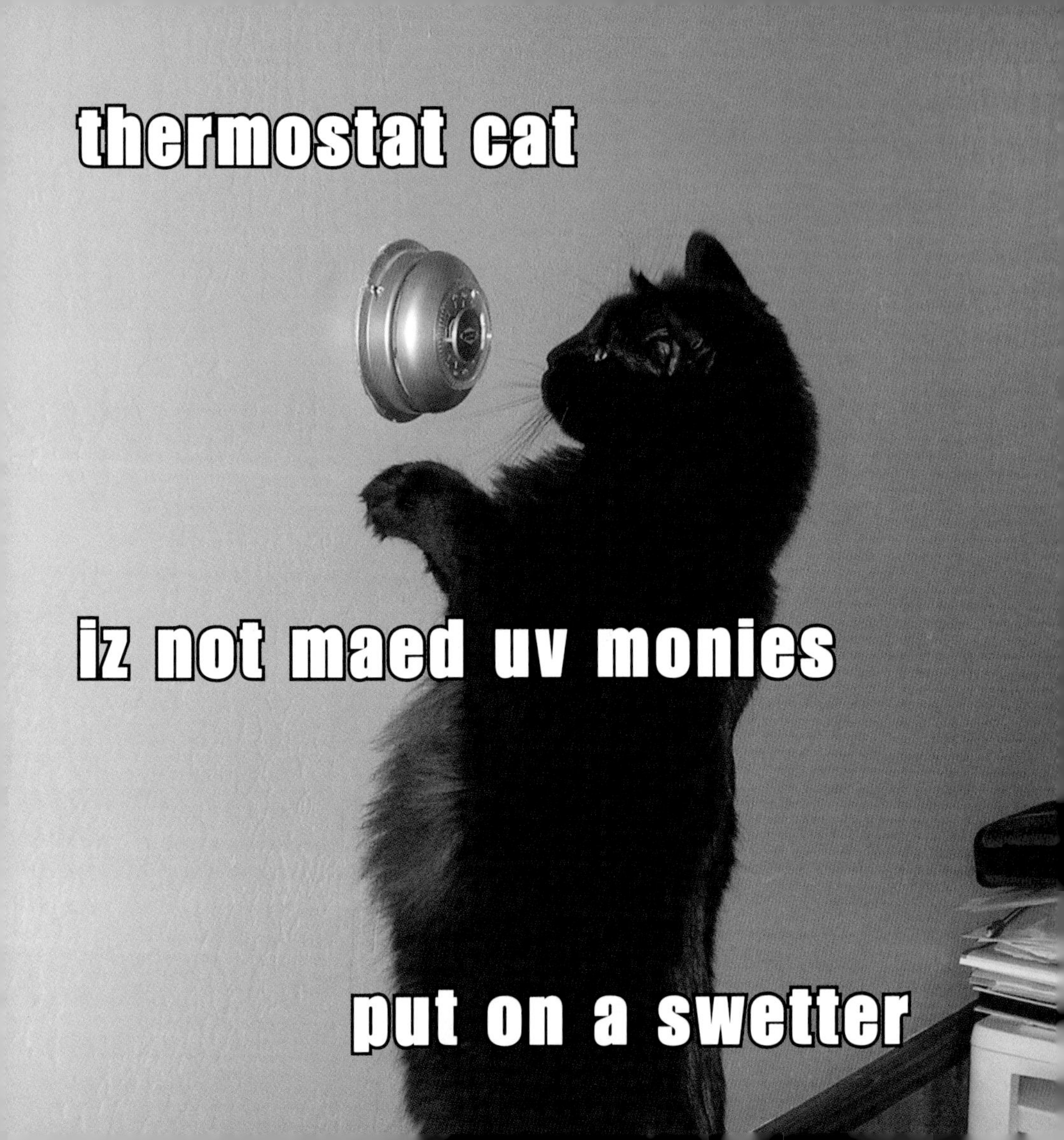
thermostat cat
iz not maed uv monies
put on a swetter

Naked Guy

reely freekin me owt

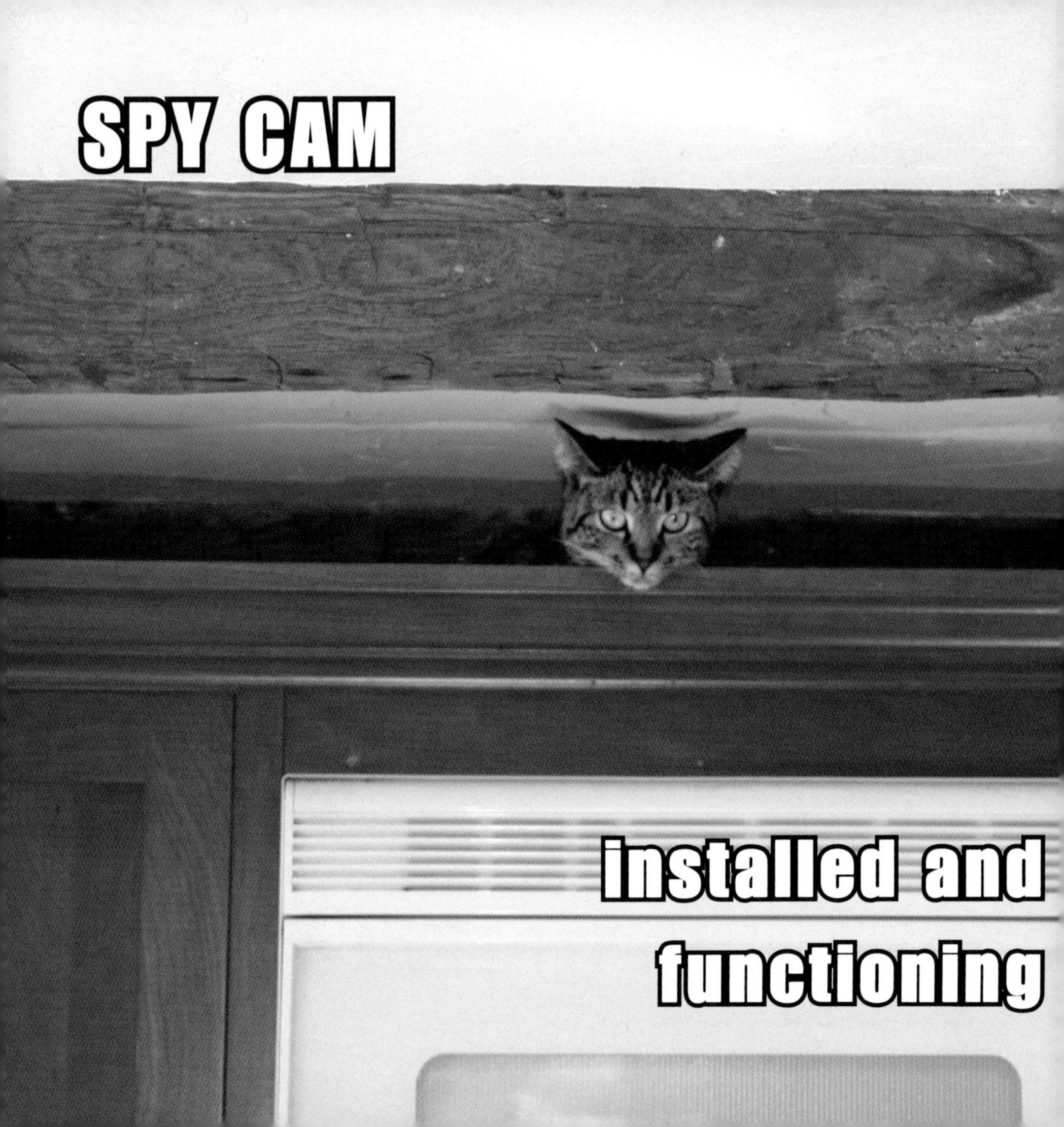
SPY CAM
installed and
functioning

im in ur hole messin wif ur hed

I C DEAD PEEPS

oh hai
been scratchin ur records

like a dj

i hope theyll be gone when i opens mah eyes

I beleeves...

in ceiling cat

I has a punkin flavor

a best friend... i has it

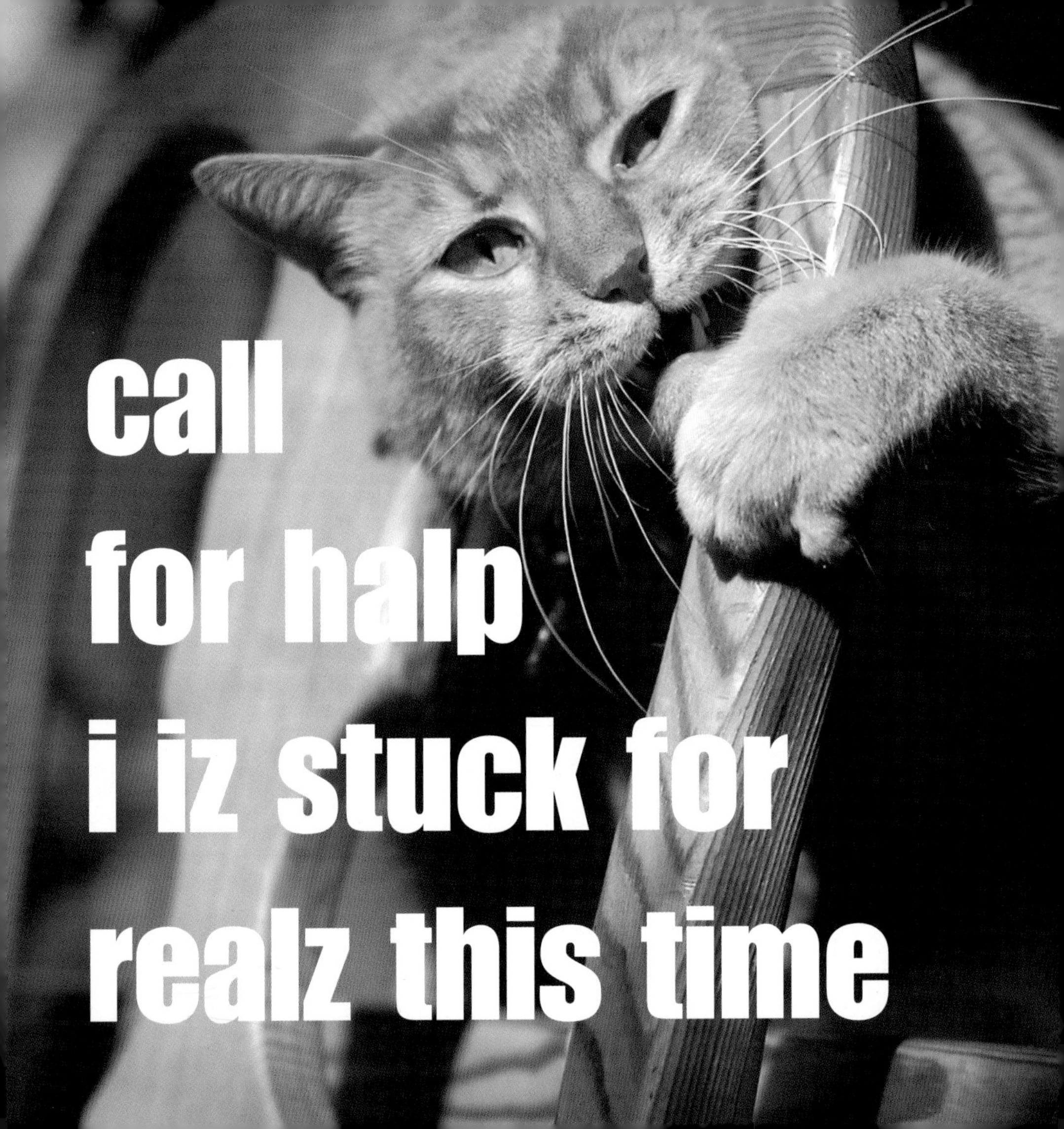
call
for halp
i iz stuck for
realz this time

invisible gui-
tar solo

I has a job interview

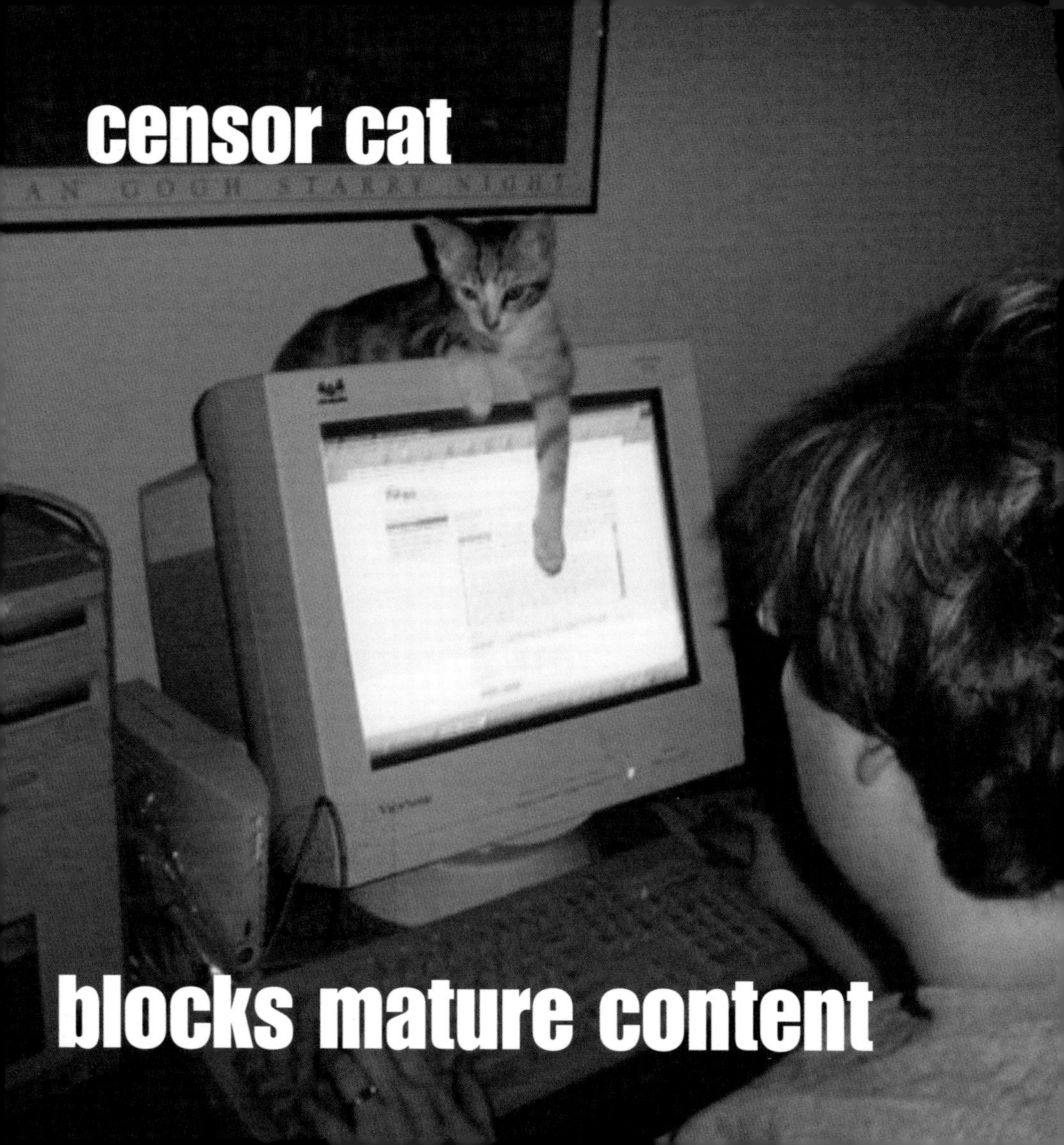
censor cat
blocks mature content

# NOM NOM NOM

used to express plezure at eating sumfing rly good.

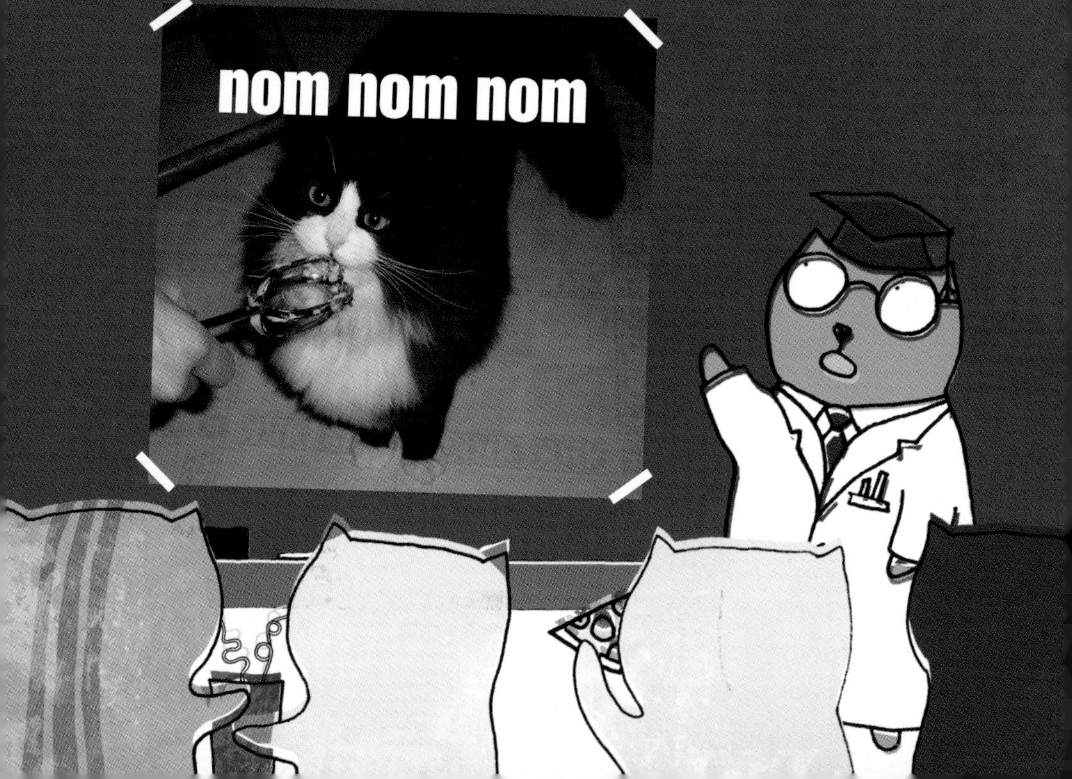

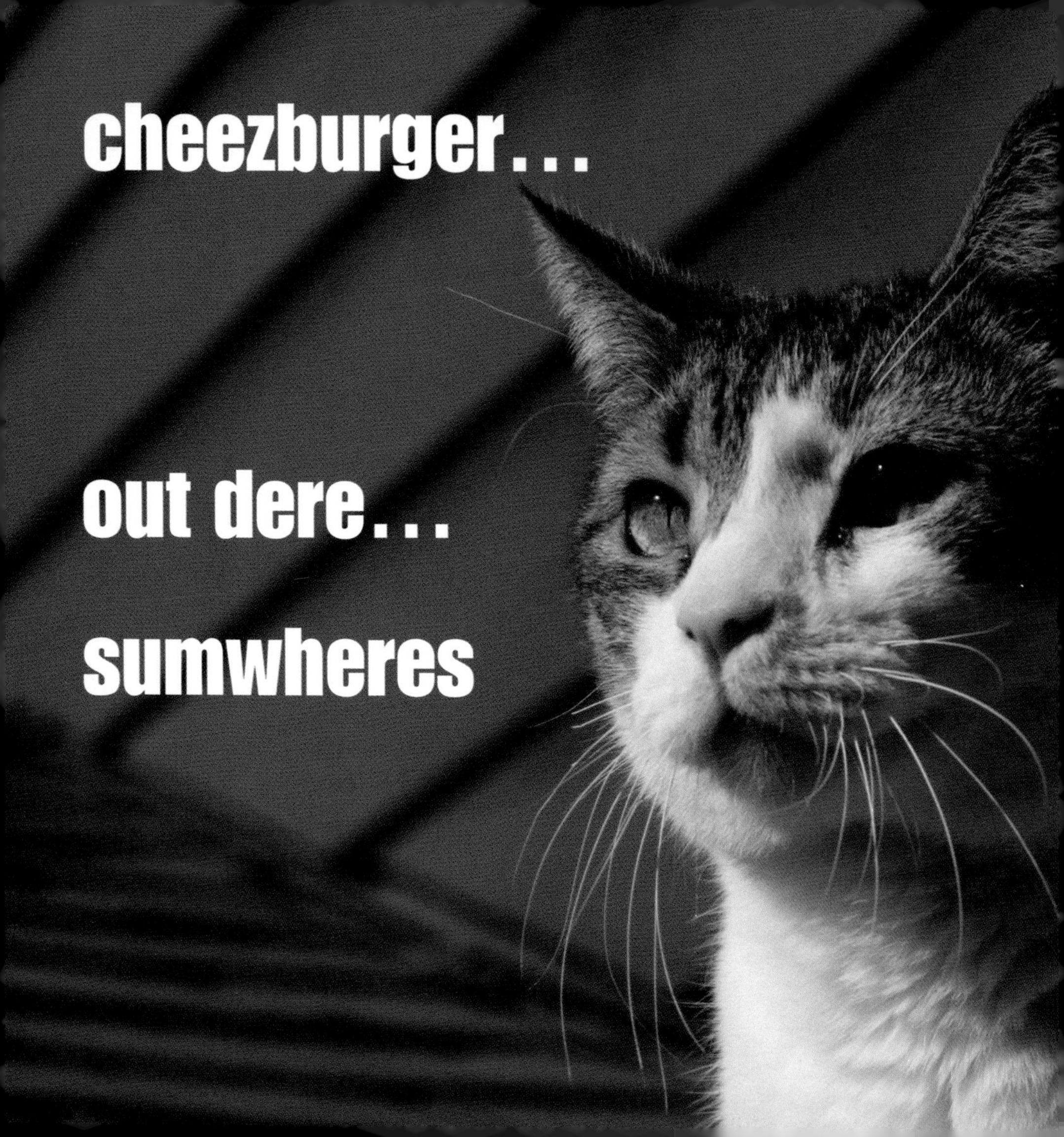
cheezburger...
out dere...
sumwheres

banana fone

ringing off teh hook

greedy cat wants it all

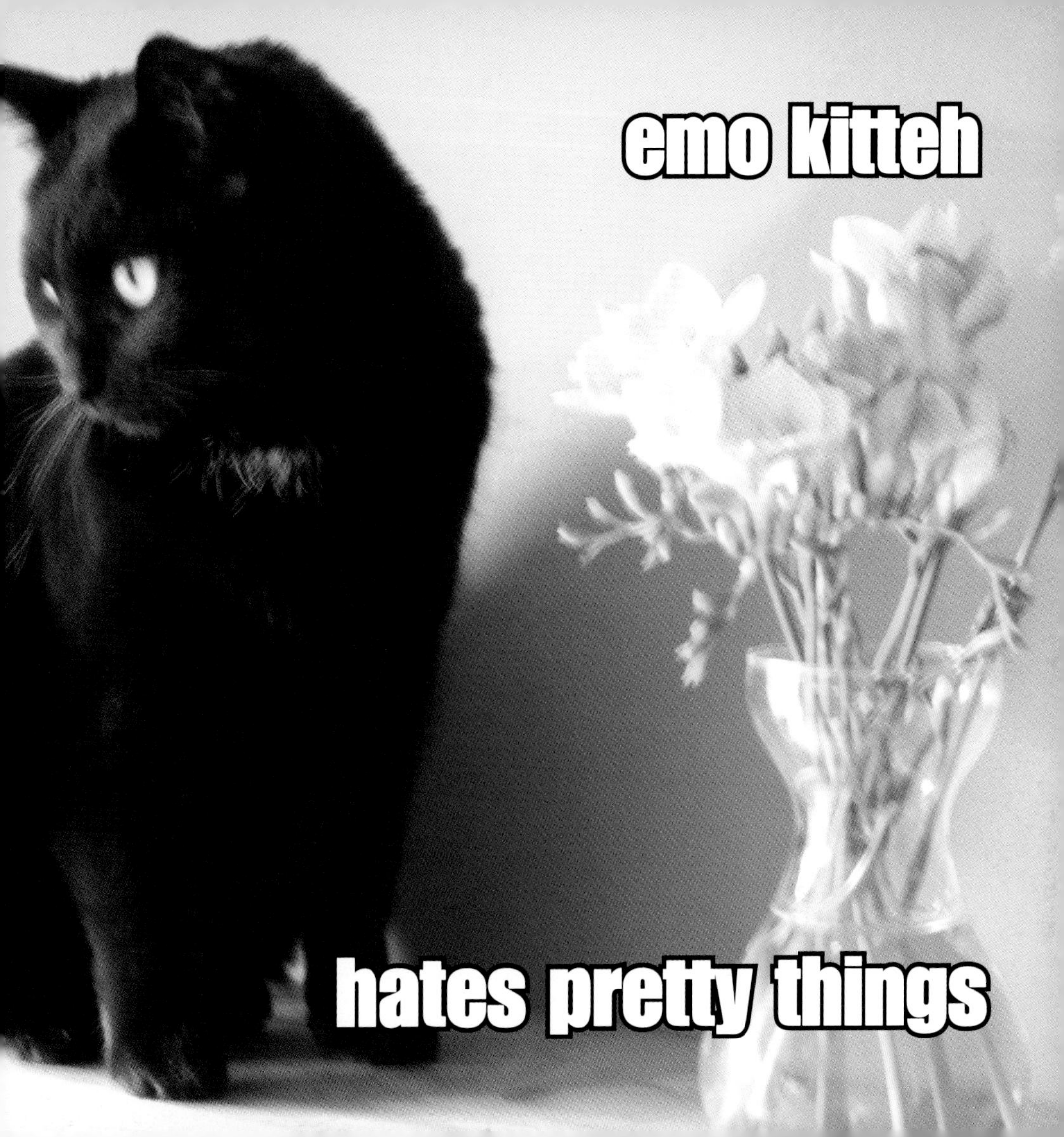
emo kitteh
hates pretty things

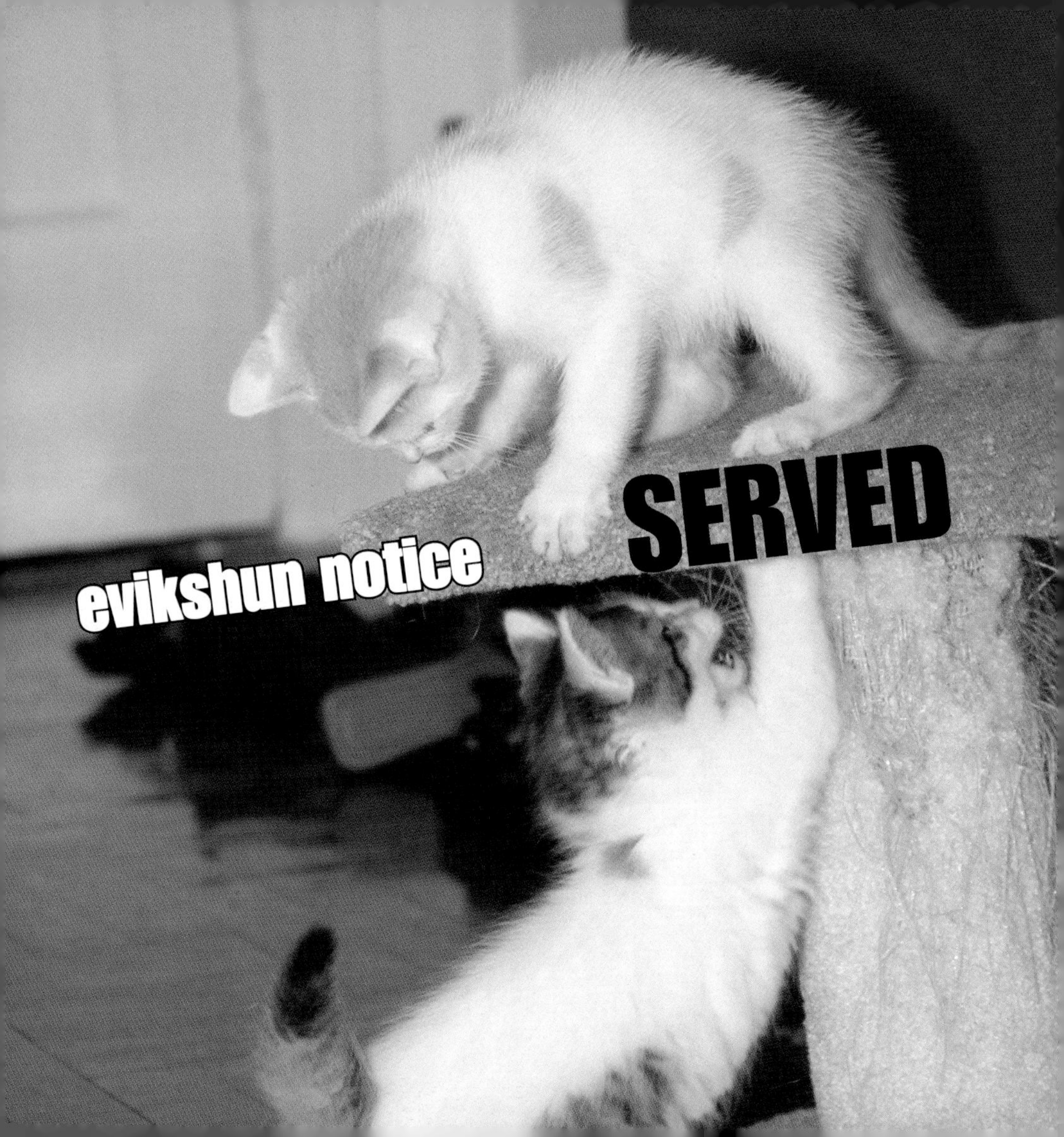
evikshun notice
SERVED

grudge cat iz still ignoring u

financial advisor cat
disapprovs of ur banking methods

HAND ME THE WRENCH!

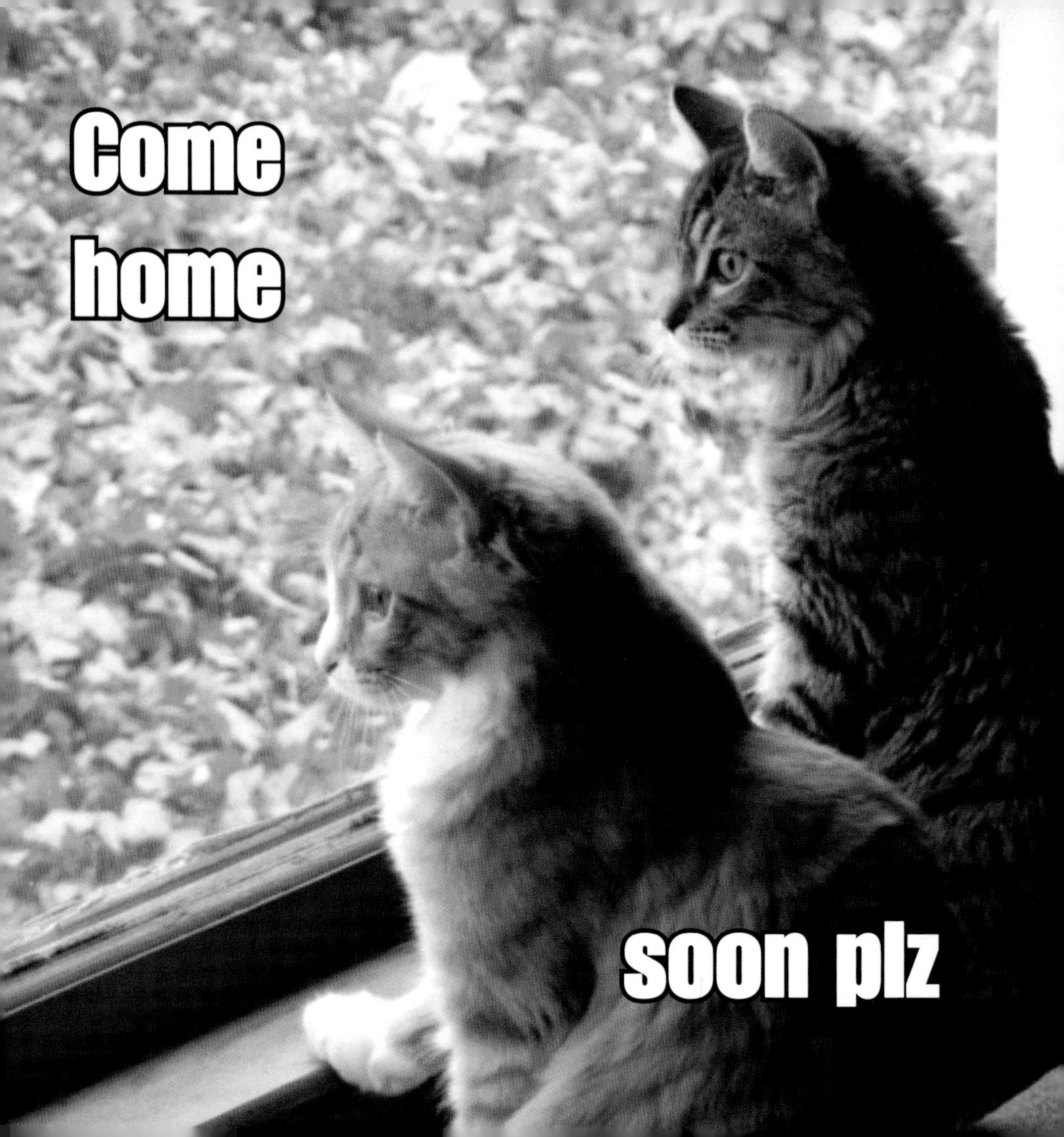
Come
home
soon plz

gps cat
sez
u lost

for a brief shining moment
parrot thought he won

evr hav the feelin ur bein watched?

Hello from ebays!

not wut u xpected?

couch kitteh

awaits ur arrival

lol

u peed ur pants

catini shaken not stirred

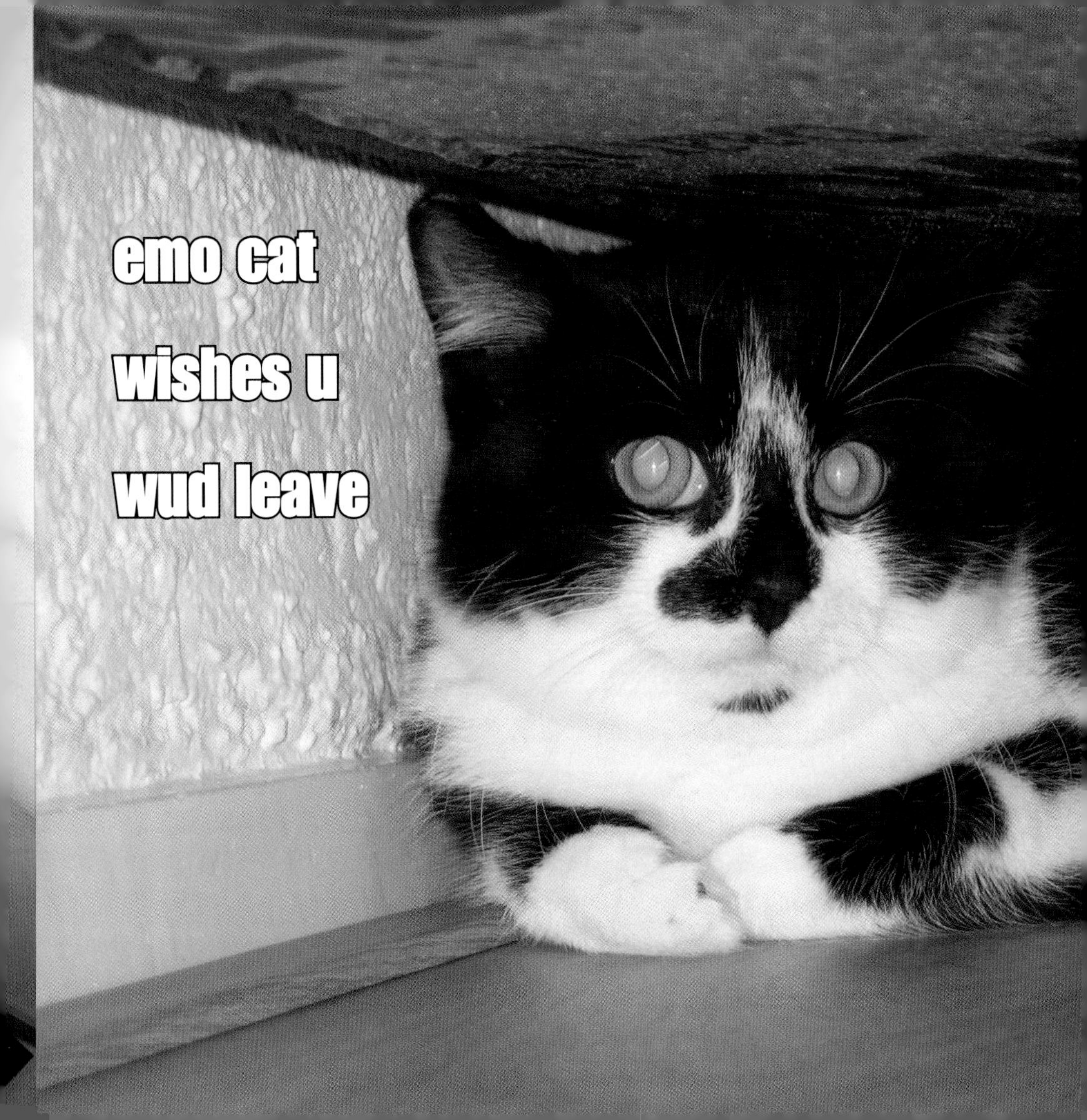
emo cat
wishes u
wud leave

i has a hat

# INVISIBLE

not visibl; not perseptubl by tha eye

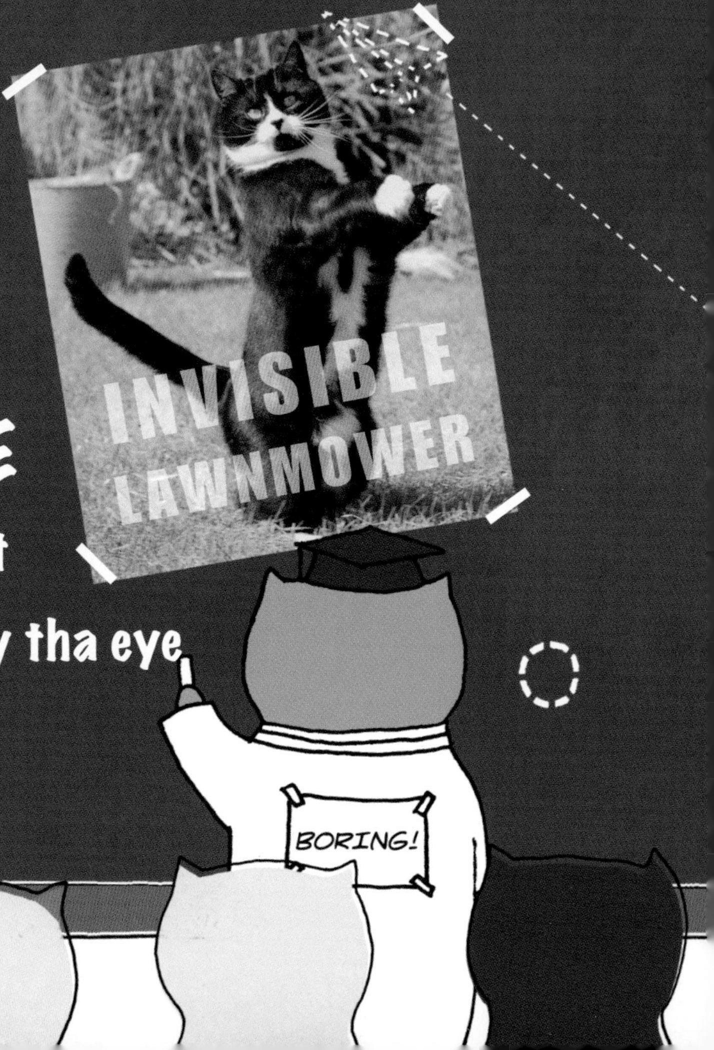


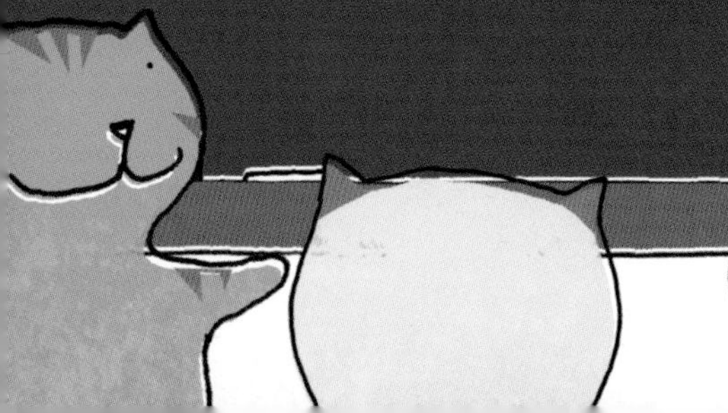

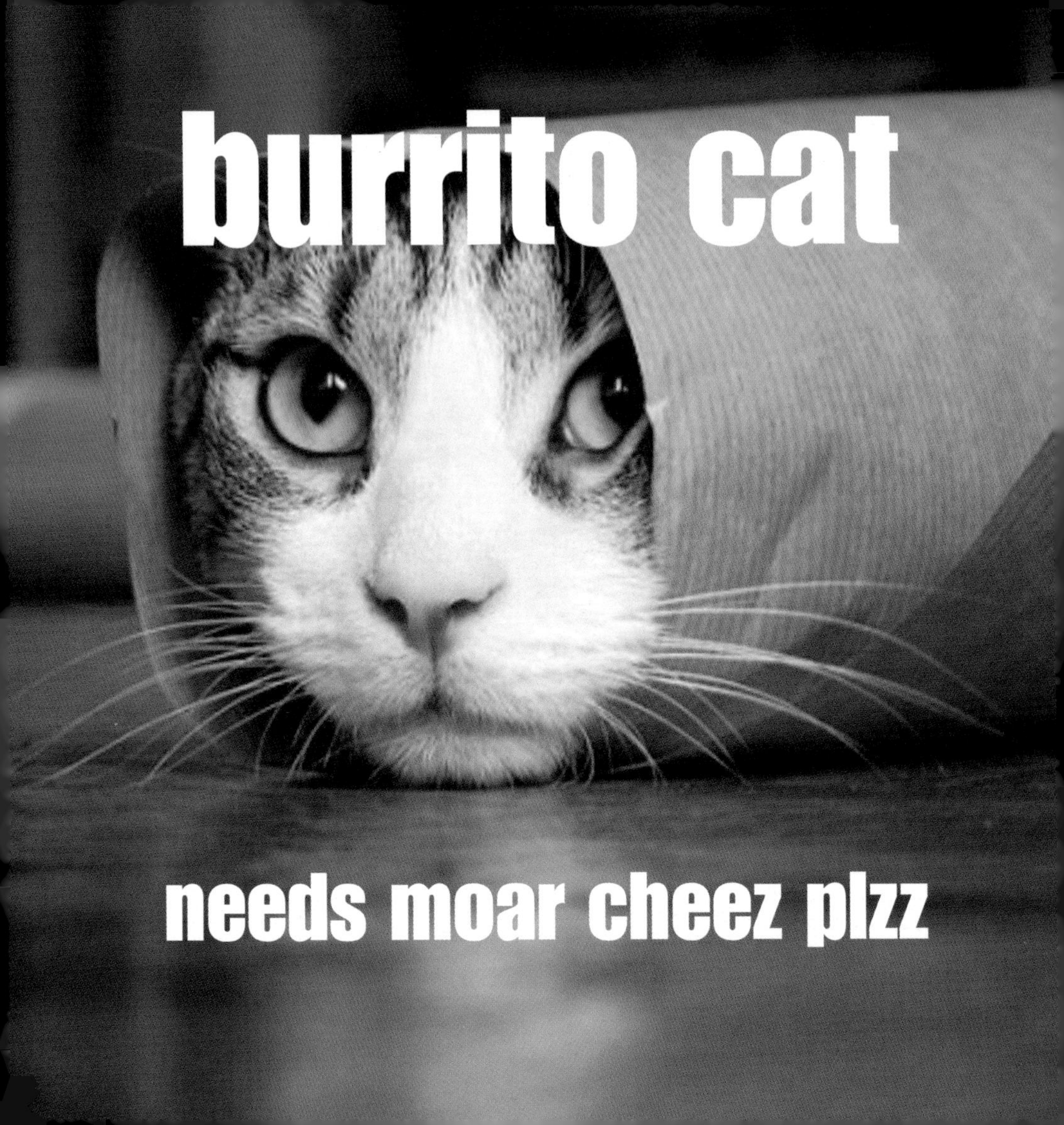
burrito cat
needs moar cheez plzz

get out

taking bath

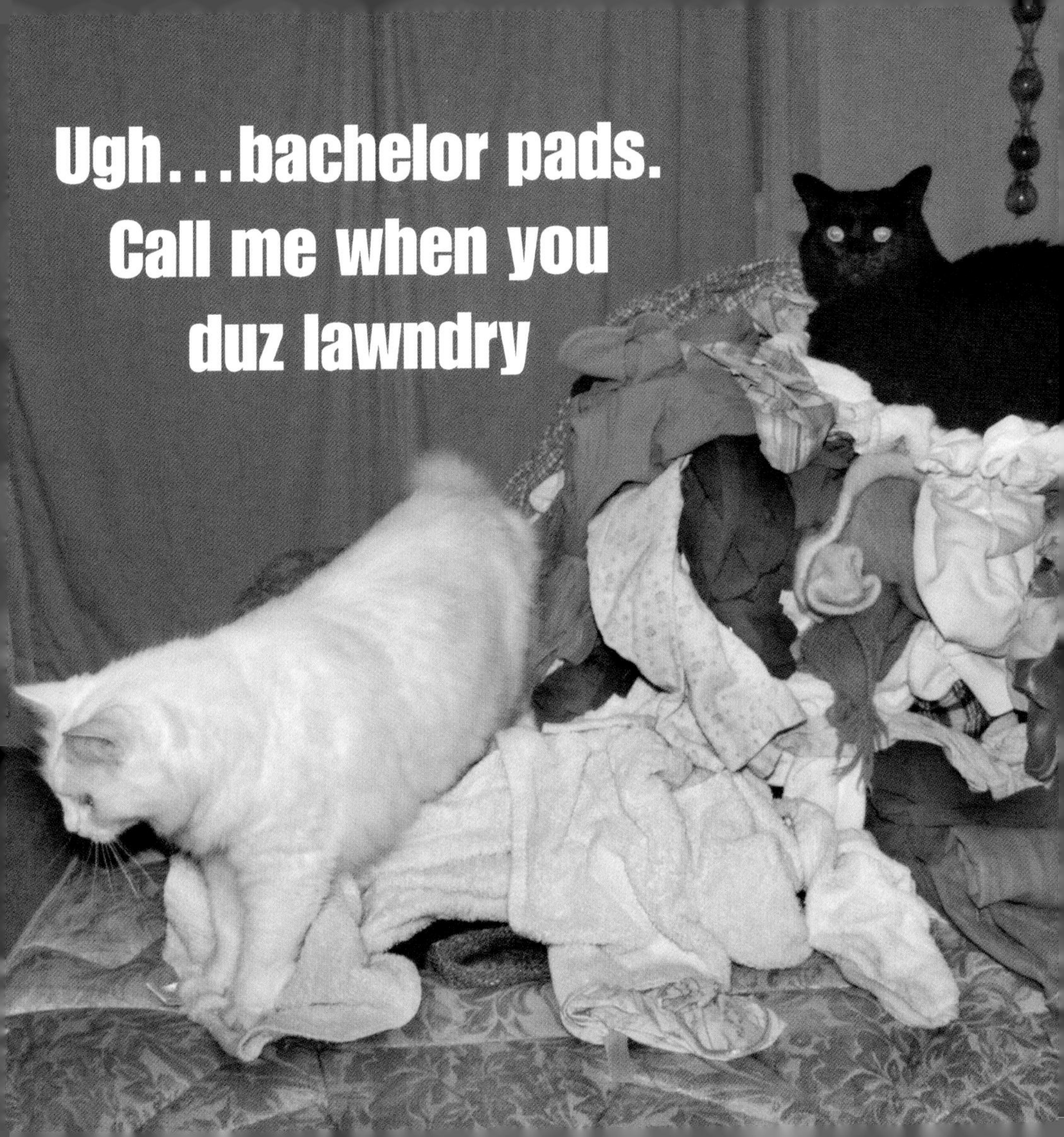
Ugh...bachelor pads.
Call me when you
duz lawndry

caffeine crash

i has it

kitteh frozen

must reboot

CAN I PLZ HAS

2 CHEEZBURGERS

3 PUGBURGERS

6 CHIKIN NUGITS

NO WAIT MAKE IT 9

insert cheezburger

doorcat

saw what u did there

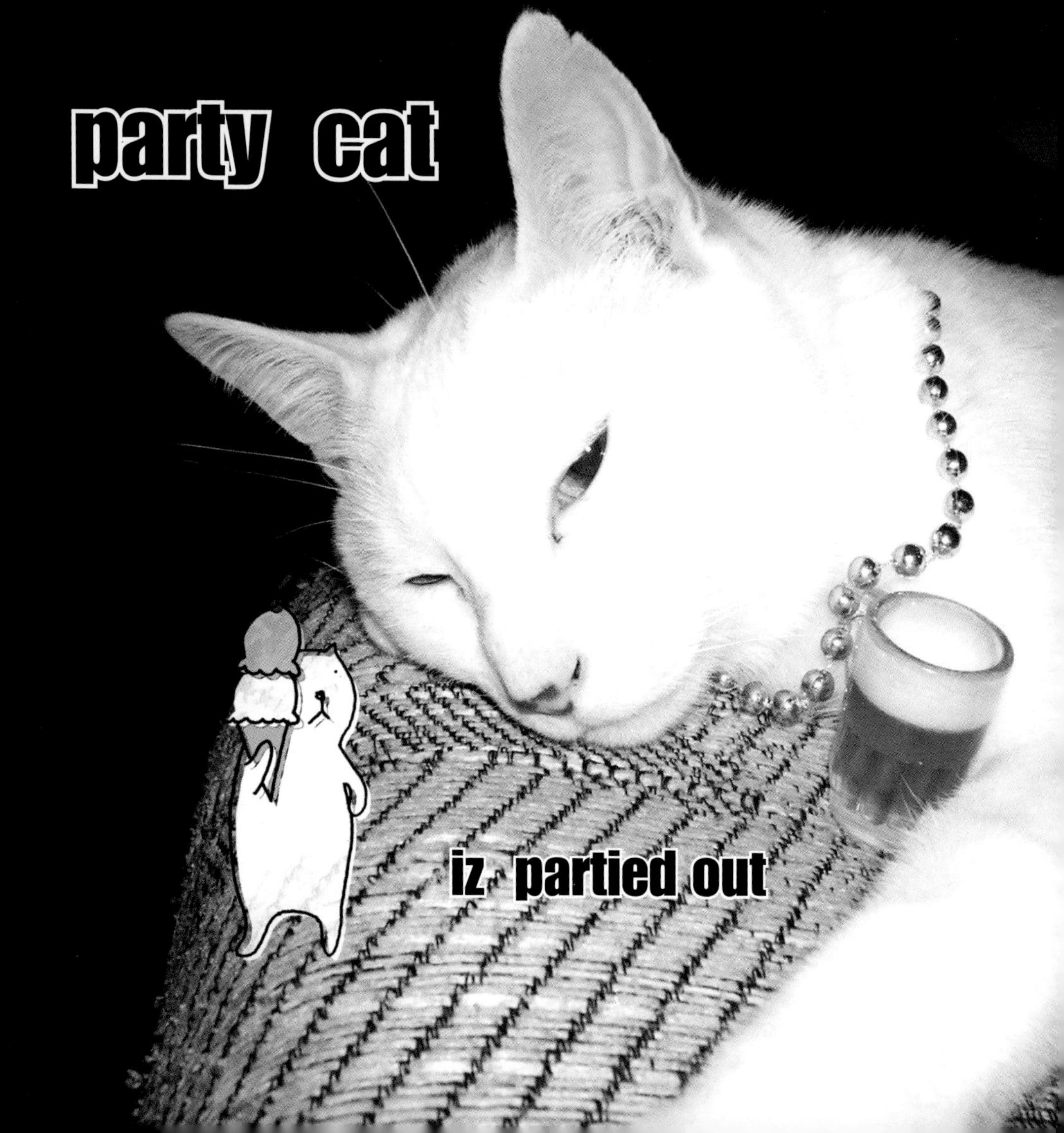
party cat
iz partied out

Made in ... 1999
© Inter IKEA ...
PQM
14
700 17238
IKEA®
0739

**kaat furry doorstop by IKEA**

designer sven fuzzybottom

cloning
ur doin it wrong
UR DOIN IT WRONG
statement to
express fail

laser eye surgery
ur doin it wrong
Facebook
ur
doin it
wrong
handpuppet
ur doin it wrong

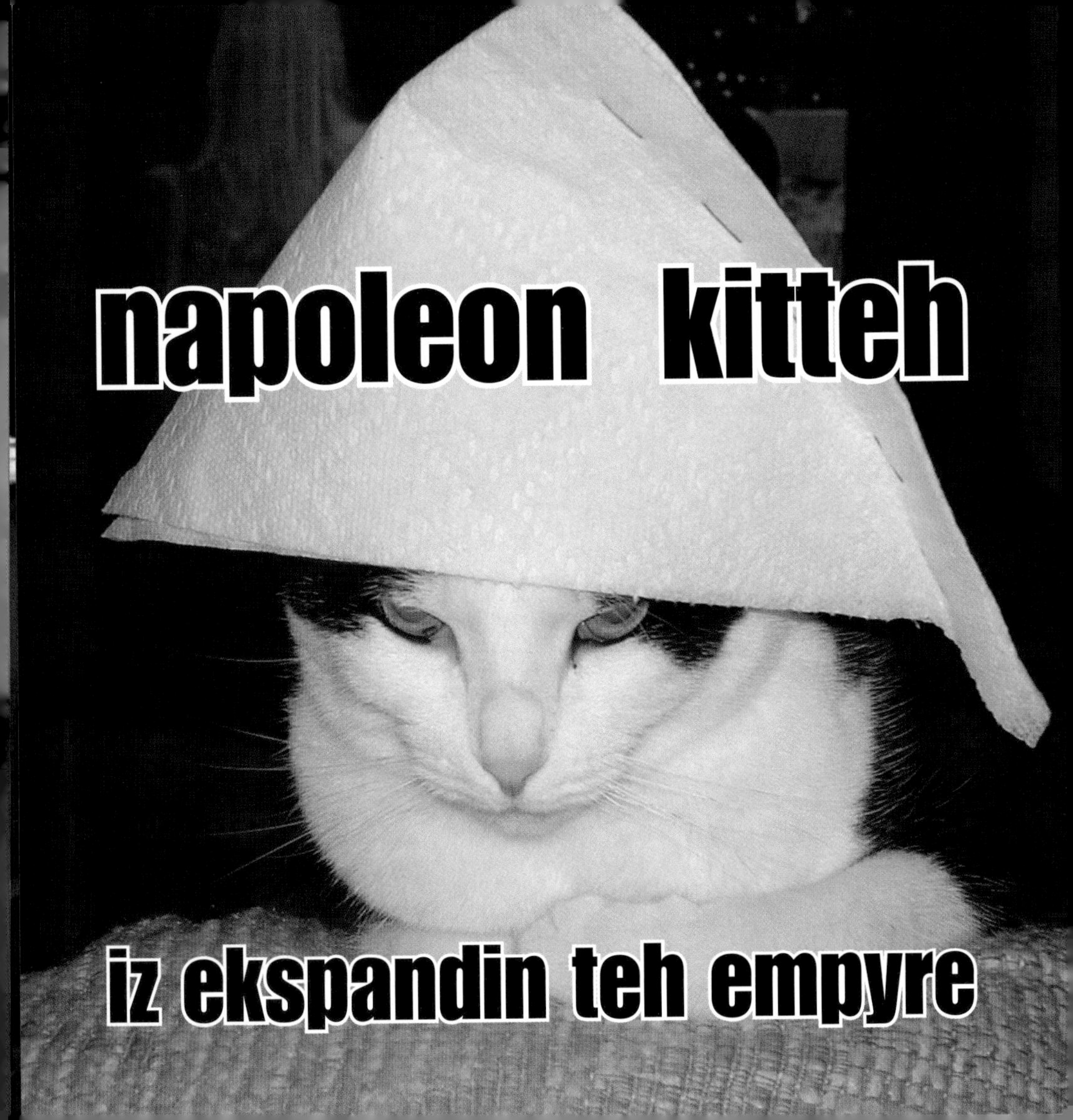
napoleon kitteh
iz ekspandin teh empyre

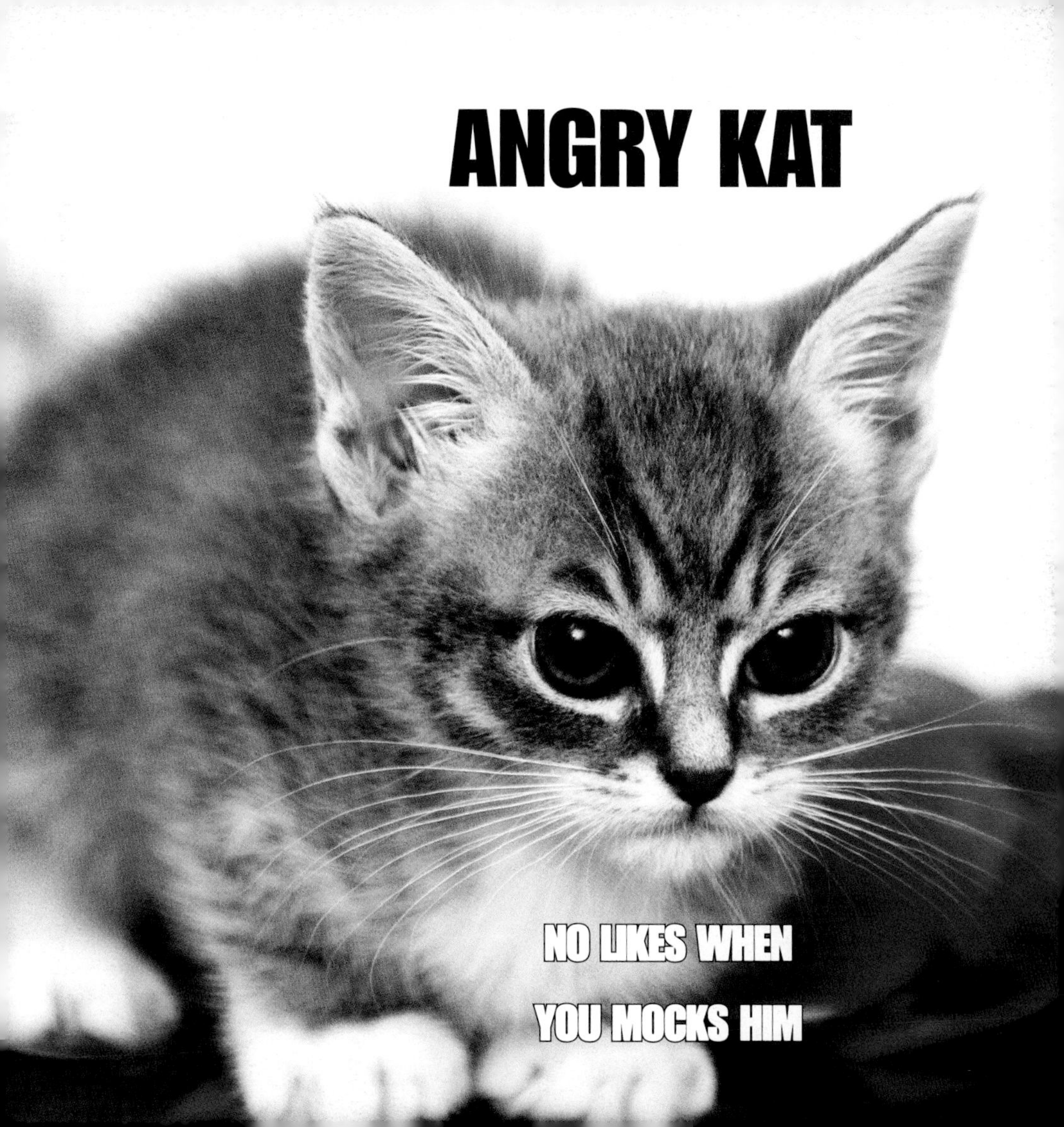
ANGRY KAT
NO LIKES WHEN
YOU MOCKS HIM

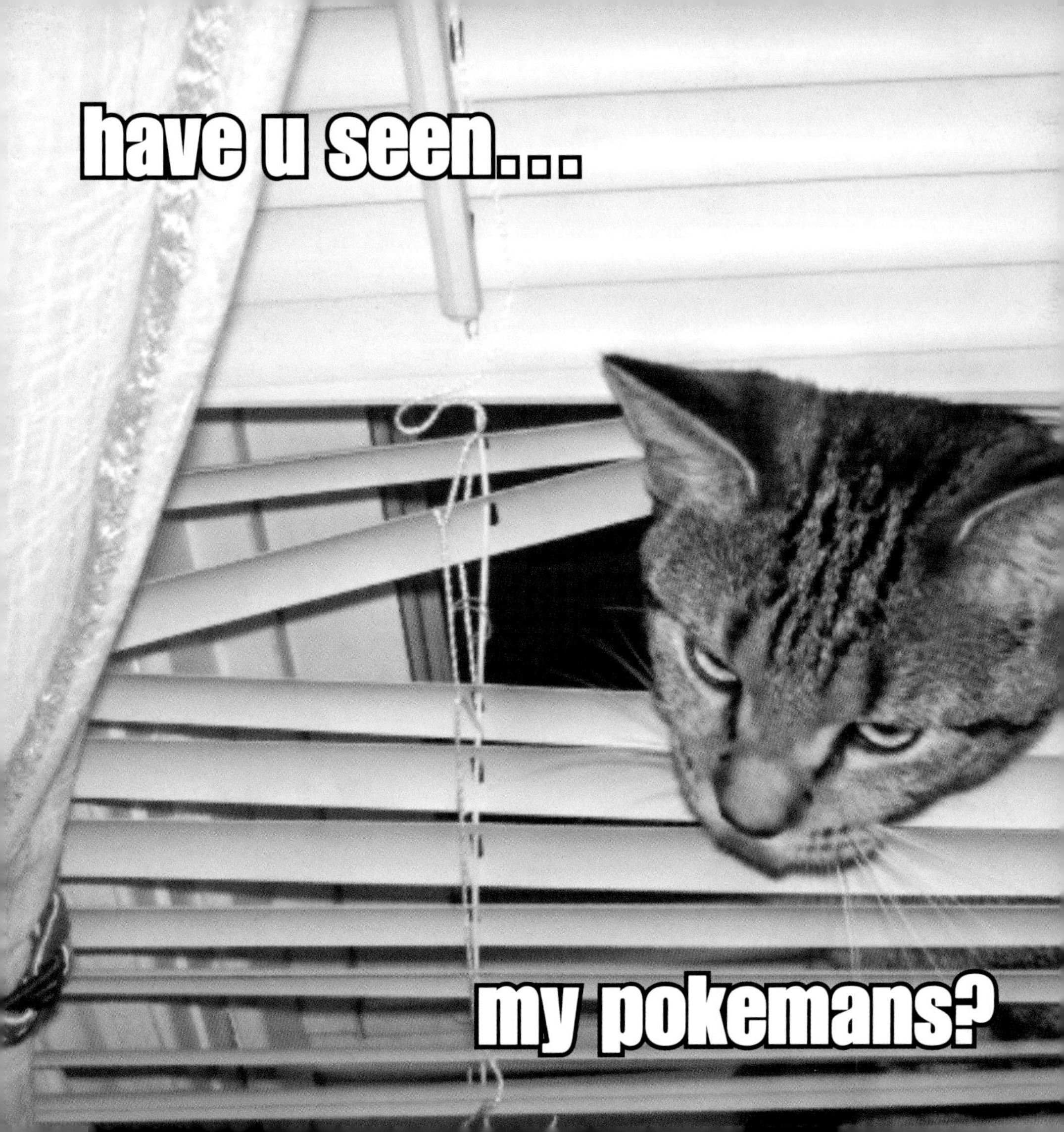
have u seen...
my pokemans?

faces

or

vase?

chek
her out

she says she's 3
look moar liek 7 to me!

conjoined kittehs

hope 2 b separated somday

no camras

kthxbai

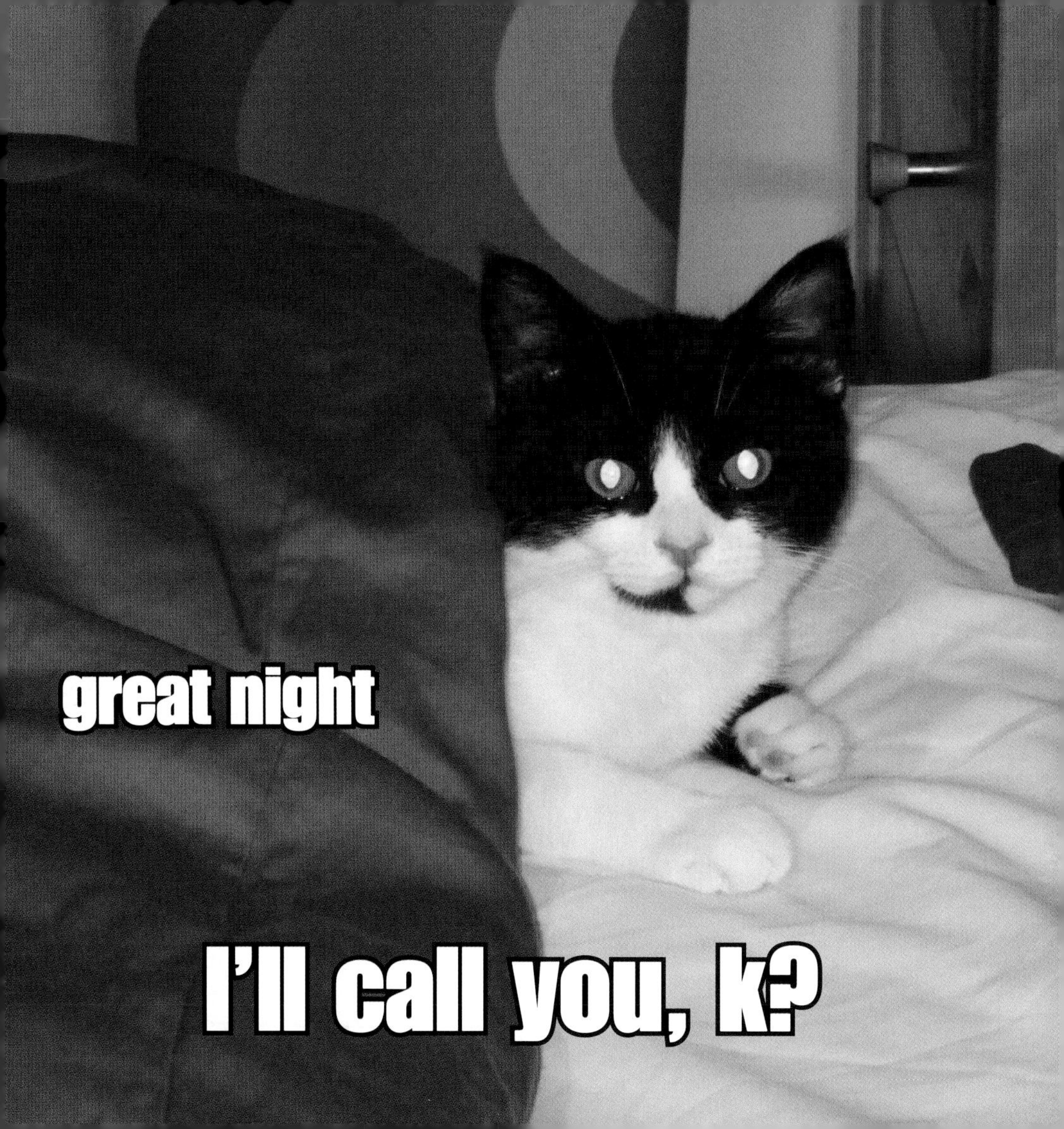
great night
I'll call you, k?

im
in ur
tube

blockin ur internets

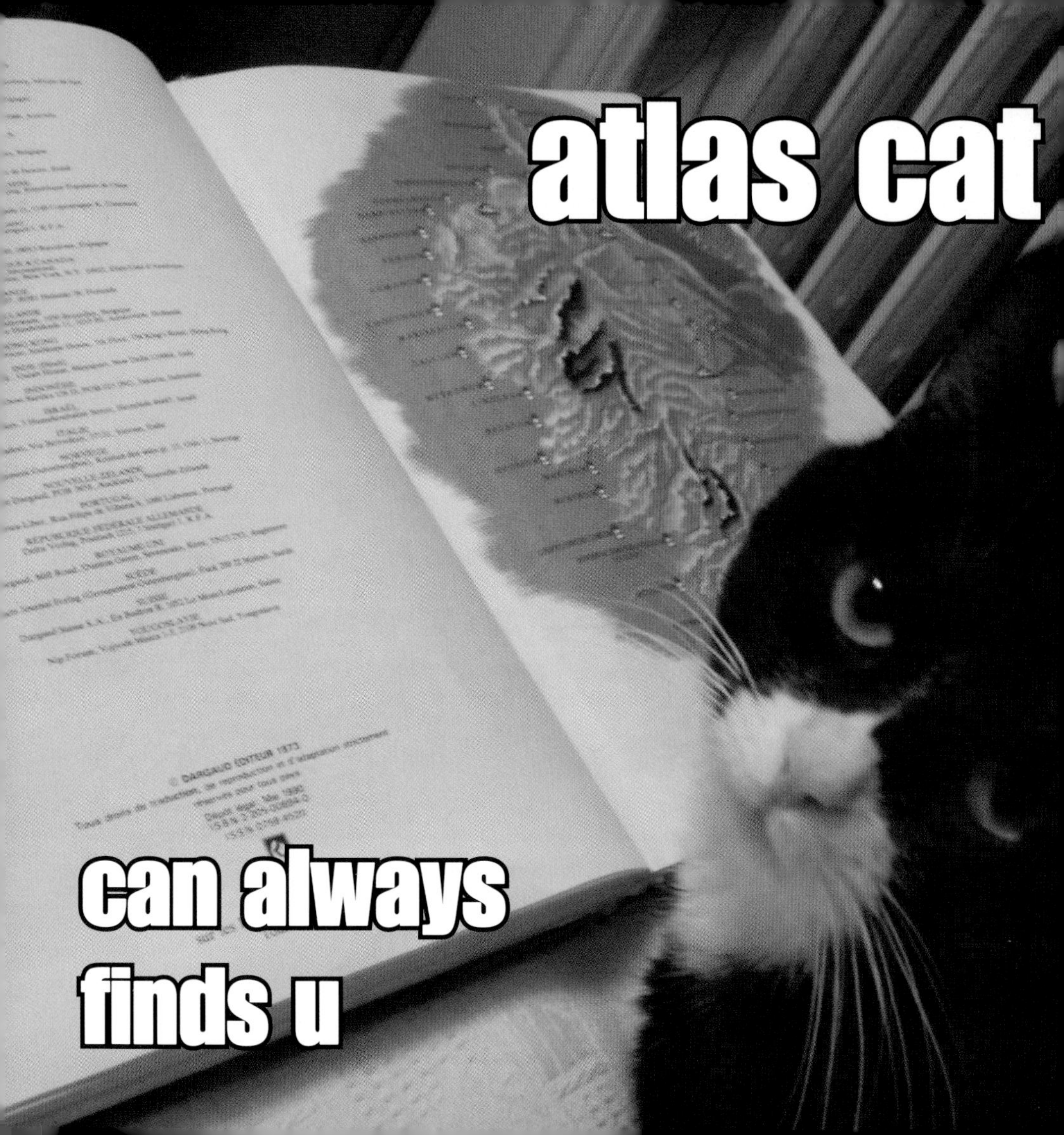
atlas cat
can always finds u

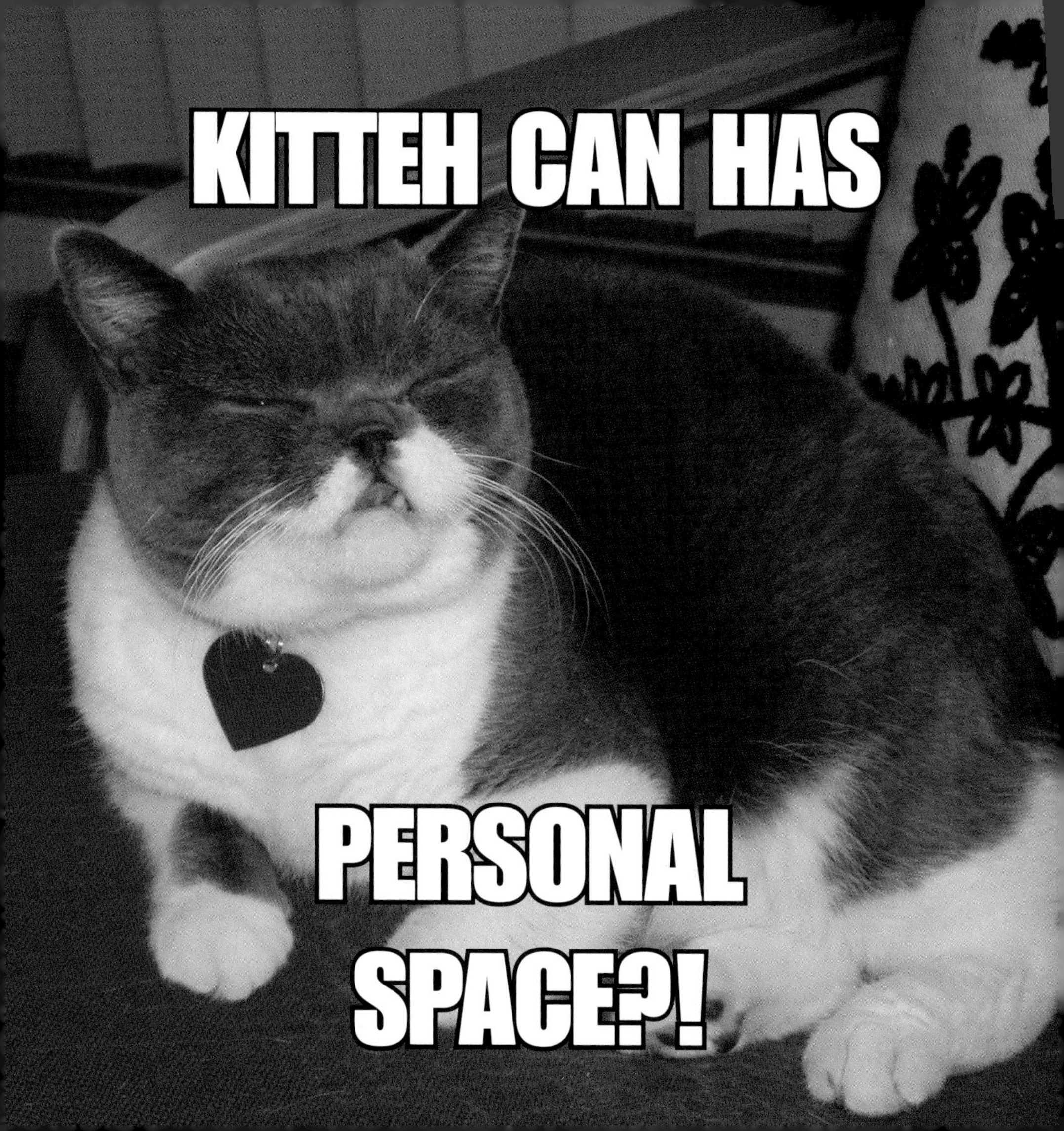
KITTEH CAN HAS
PERSONAL
SPACE?!

**where mah cheezburger?!**

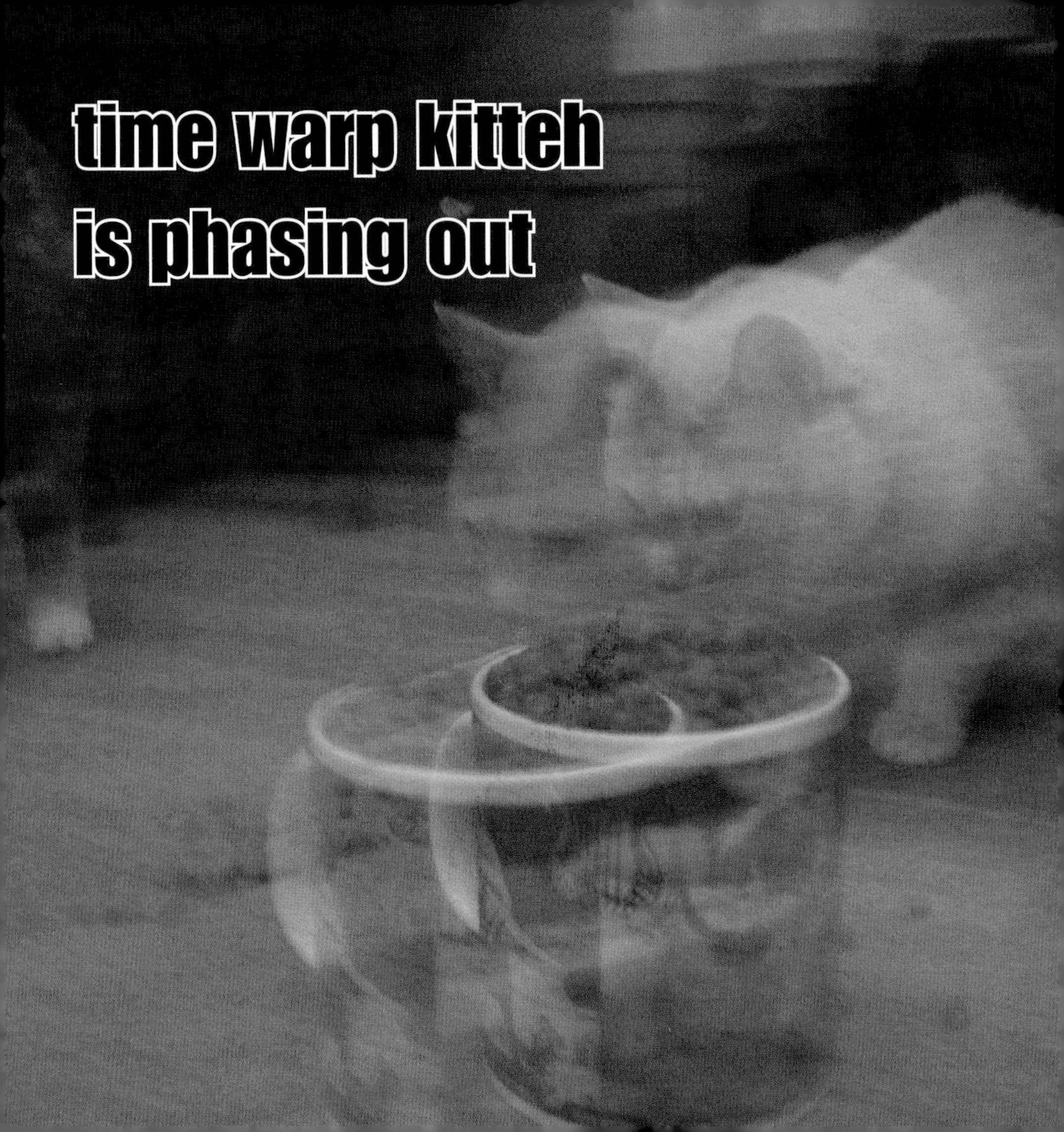
time warp kitteh
is phasing out

I tink we haz a mowse problum...

This won't end up on the internet will it?

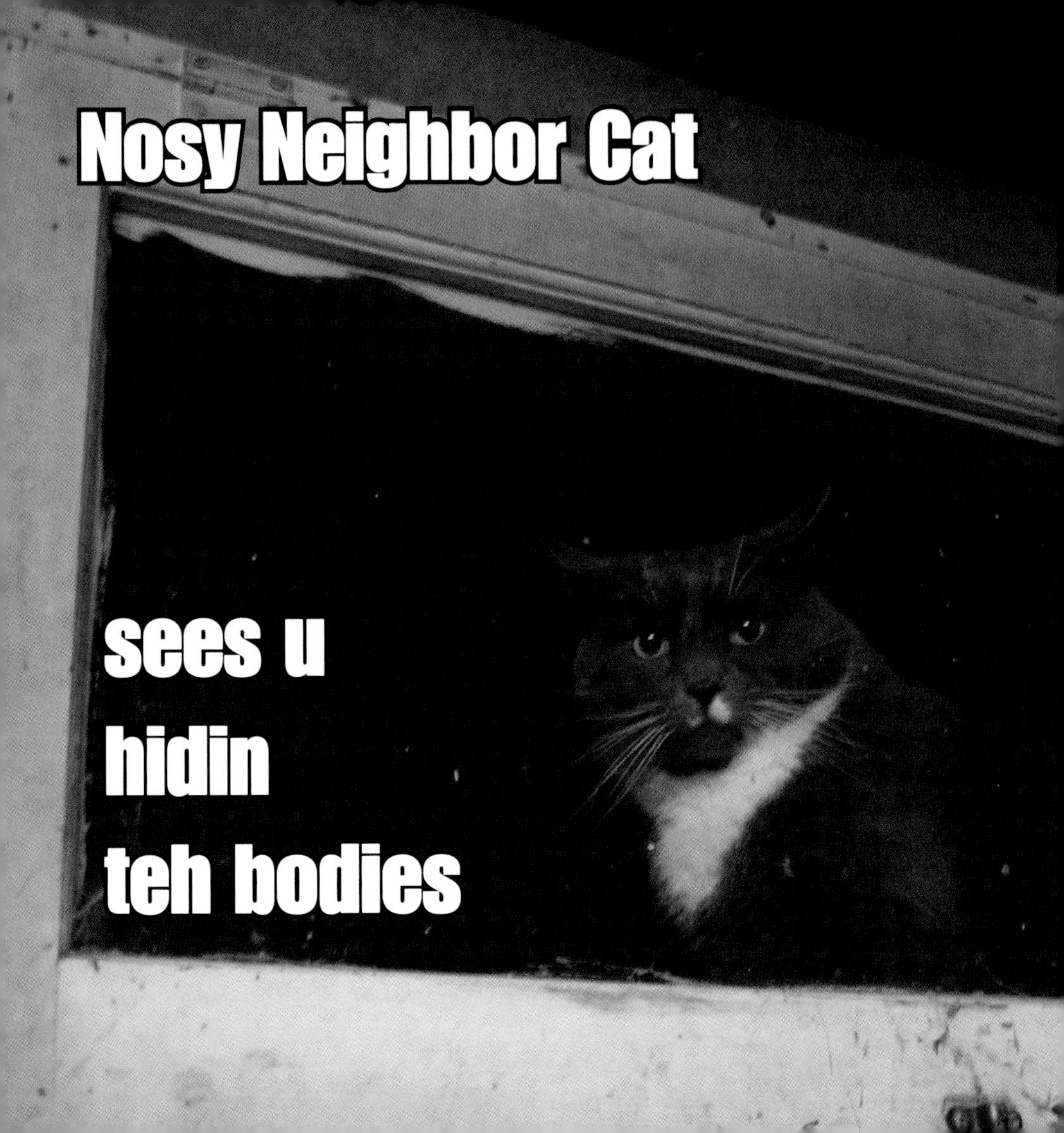
Nosy Neighbor Cat
sees u
hidin
teh bodies

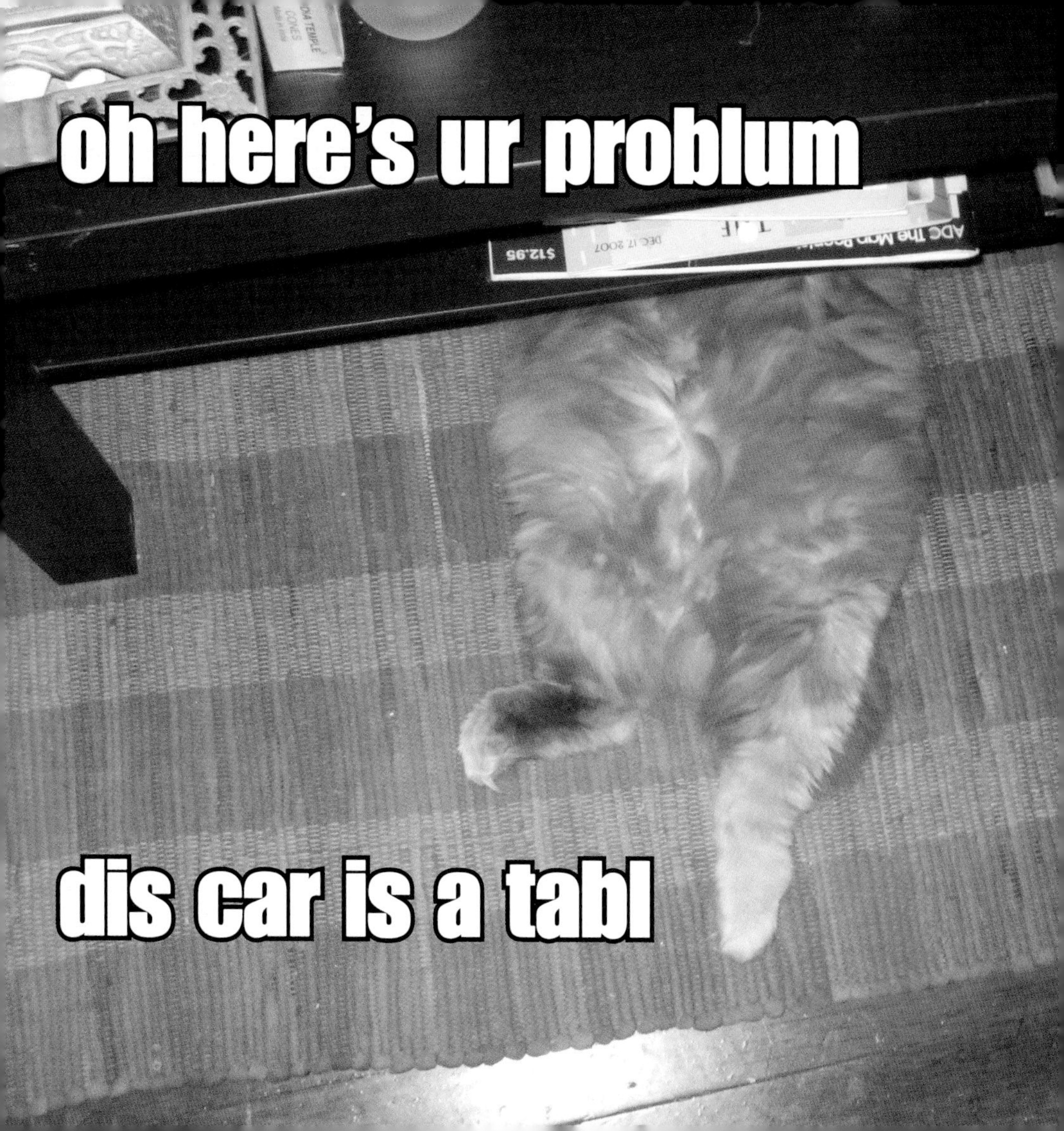
oh here's ur problum
dis car is a tabl

after face lift

u do mah nose.

dis doesn't concern u

move along

nite nite bunneh

c u in teh mornin!

DIS A JOEK RITE?

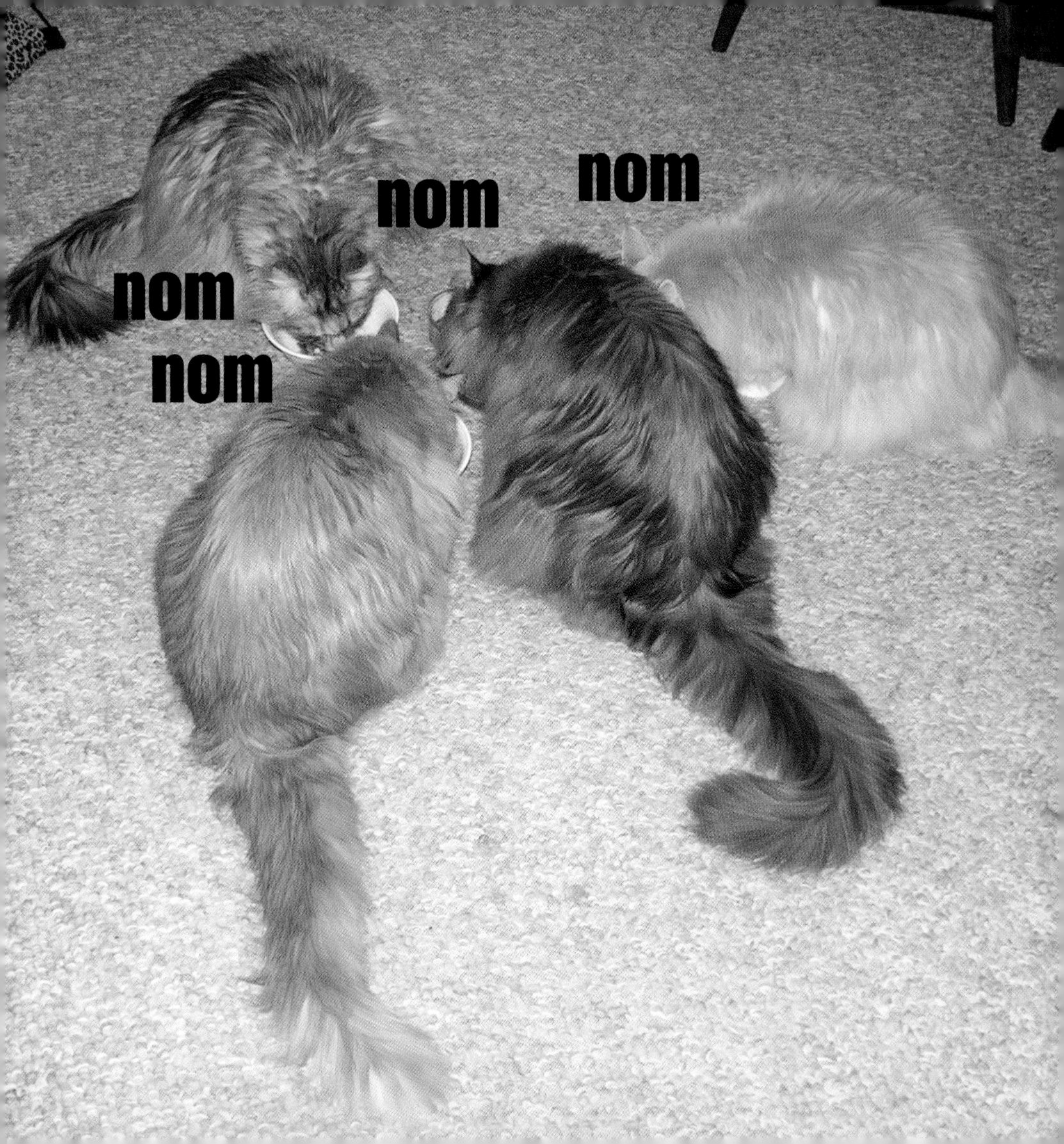
nom
nom
nom
nom

DIS NOT RIGHT KIND

BUT I EETED ANYWAY

going
somewheres?

o ur floor
so much awe-
sum!!!1!

litez
poken me
all over

IM IN UR GARDEN

SCARIN UR KIDS

IN UR —
teh kittehs iz
alwayz in
ur sumthing

I regret to
inform you
that

ll:p[[[[[[[[[[[
[[[[[[[[[[[[[

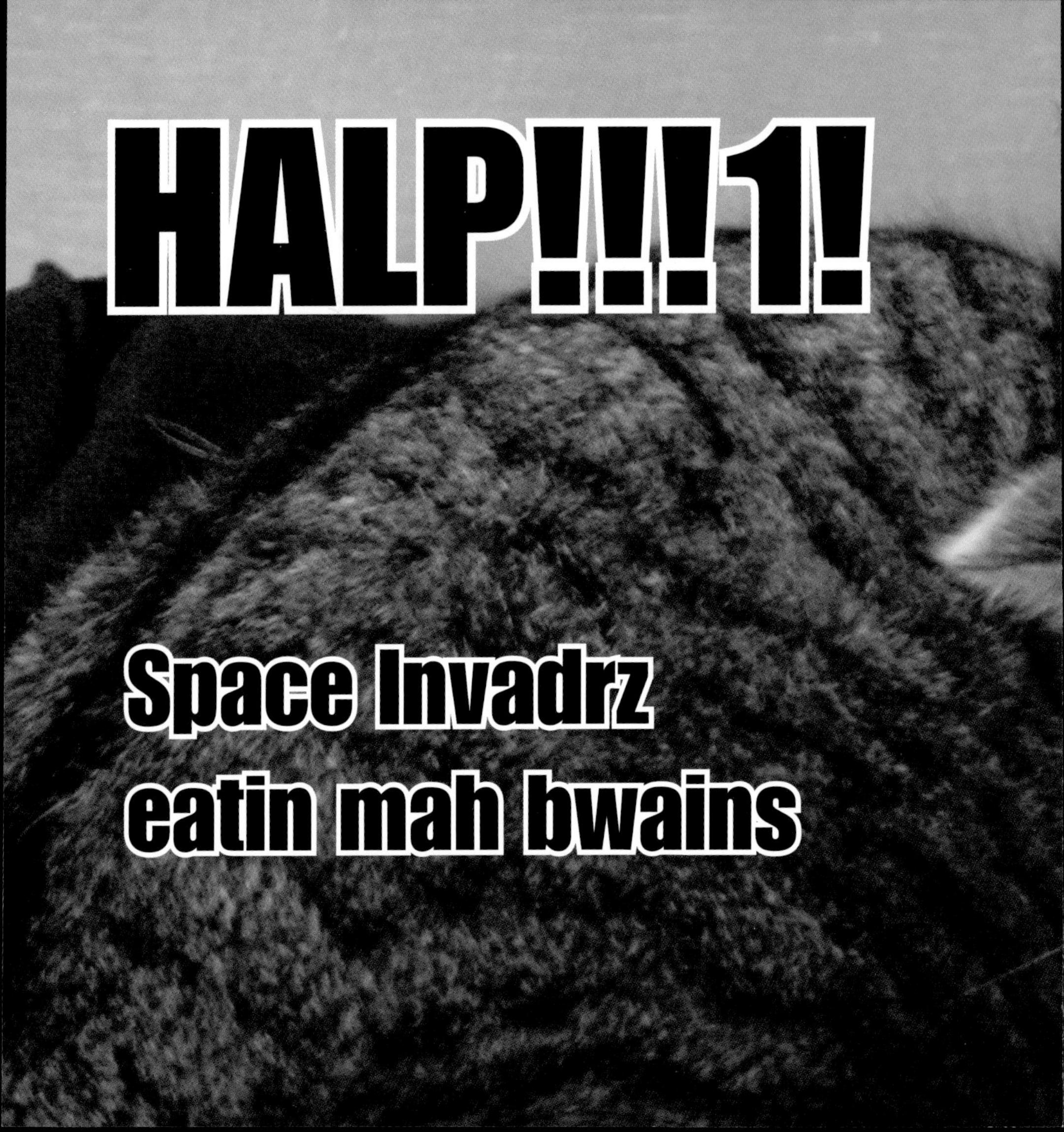
HALP!!!1!
Space Invadrz
eatin mah bwains

NEED MOAR HOTPOCKETS!

NO.

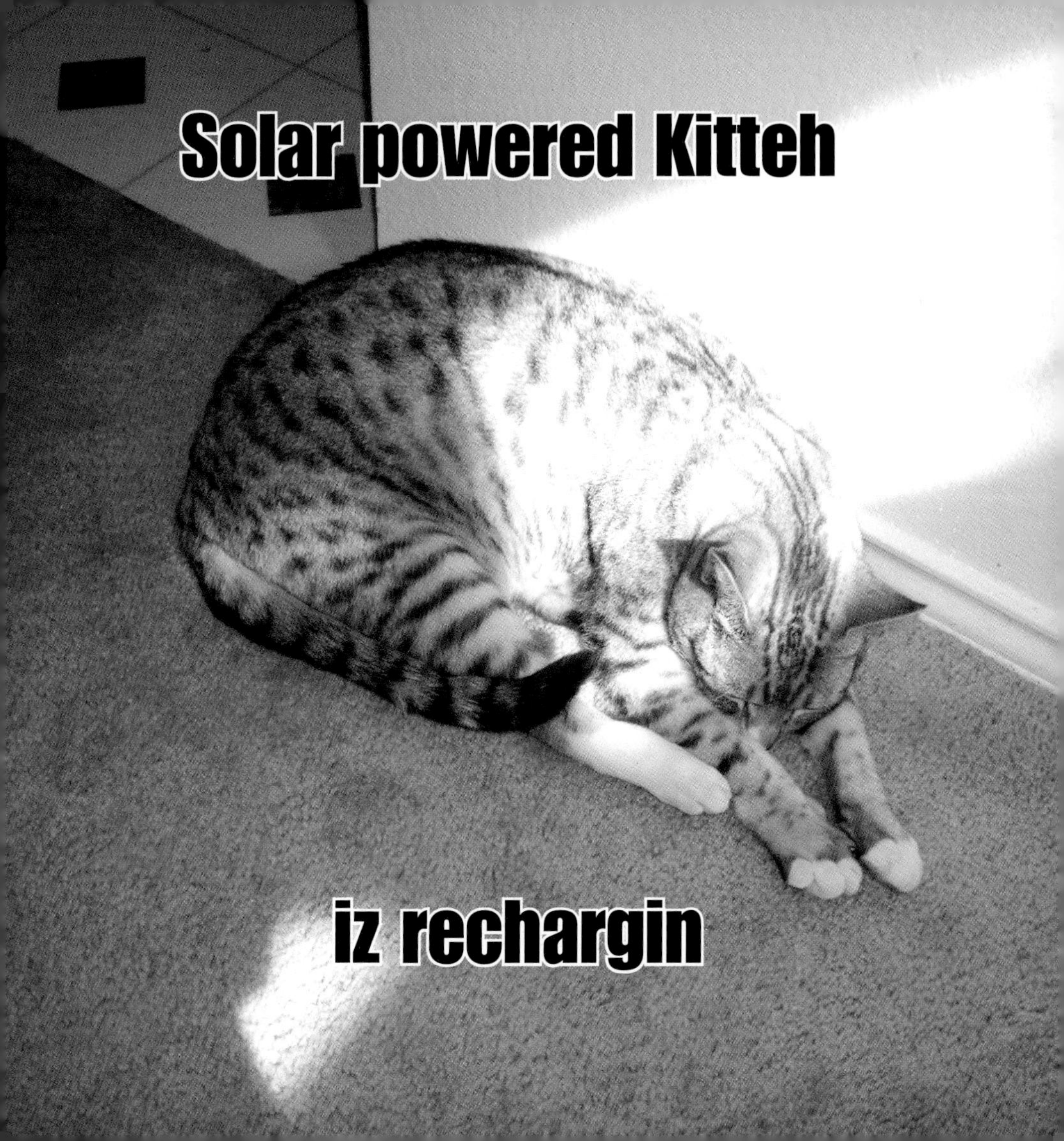
Solar powered Kitteh
iz rechargin

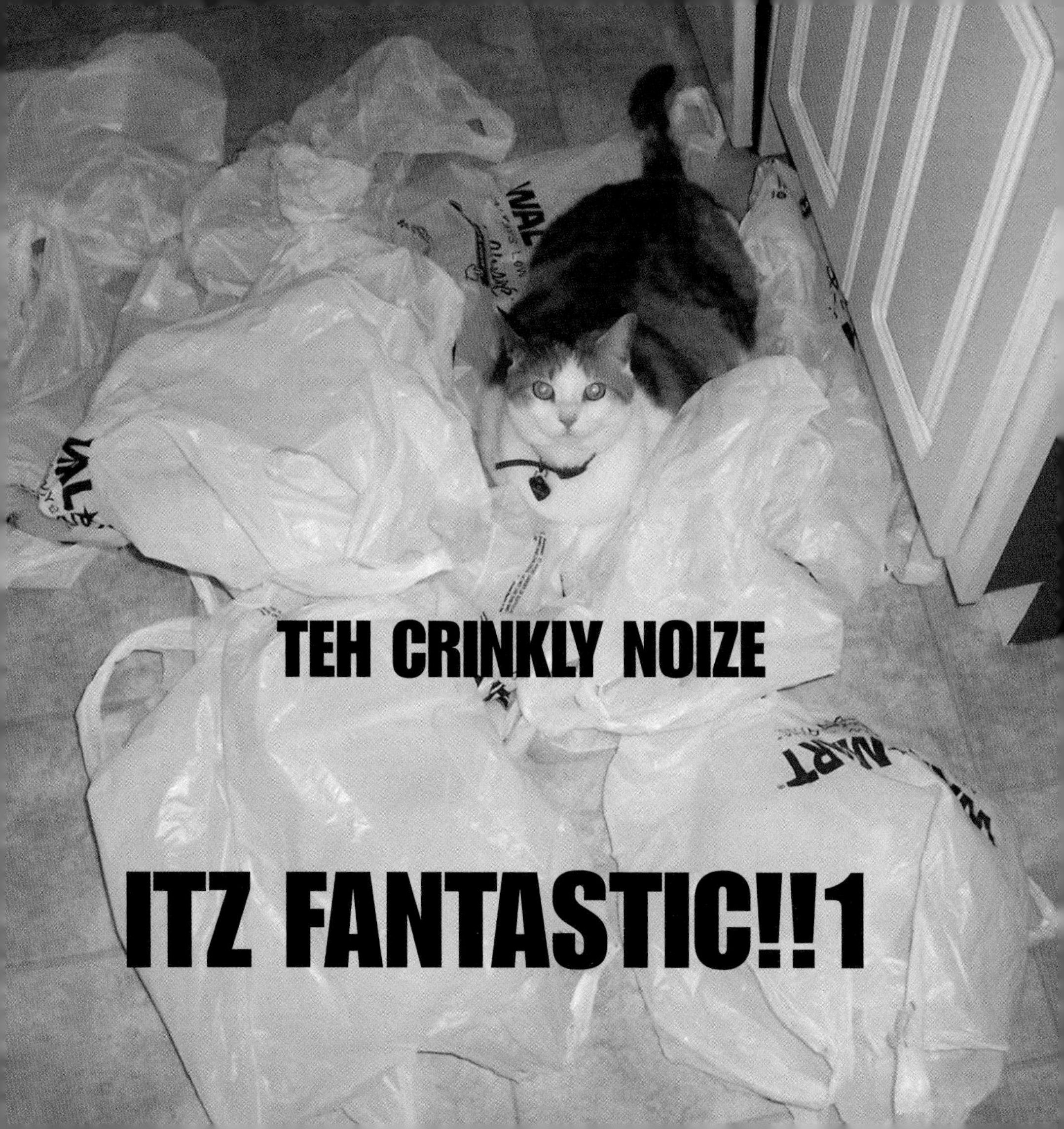
TEH CRINKLY NOIZE
ITZ FANTASTIC!!1

**new
happy meal
toyz**

**iz been in
there
for dayz**

papr
covers rock

polygraph kitteh

detects deception

SIDE EFFECTS INCLUDE:
MOOD SWINGS
LOSS OF APPETITE
HAIR LOSS

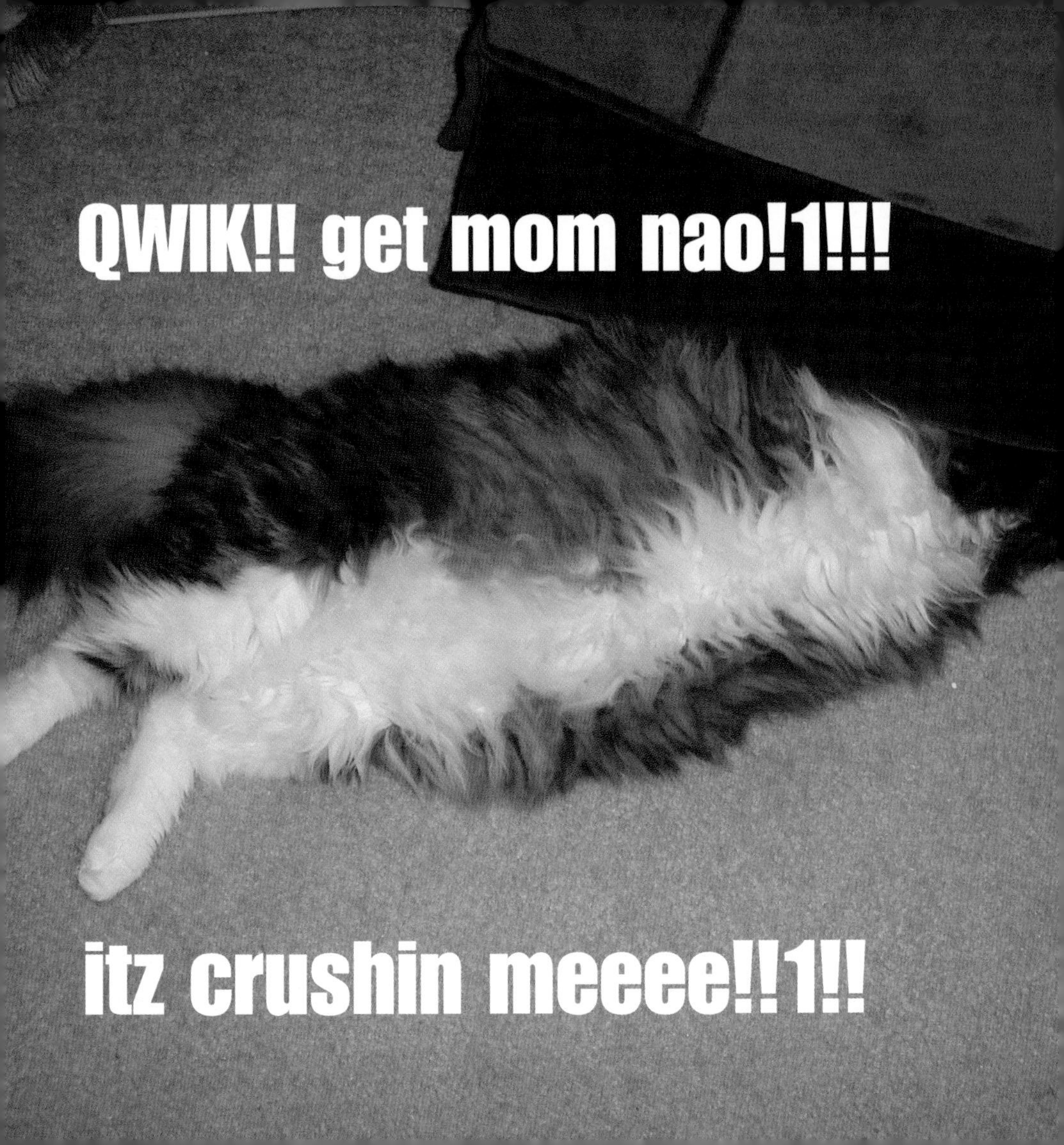
QWIK!! get mom nao!1!!!
itz crushin meeee!!1!!

relaxashun
ur doin it rite

MAIM

STUN

sleep...

...i needz it

smug kitteh

iz pleased wit
own acheevments

ceiling cat iz watching u
CEILING CAT
omnomnishent kitteh who lives in ur ceiling and observs ur persunal habitz

i darez yu to kross

no i darez yu to kross

Those who can't do...

nap.

The Teacher's PLANNER

you godda

roll wiv it

Iz stuck. Bring hunny.

To get prey...

...must be
liek prey

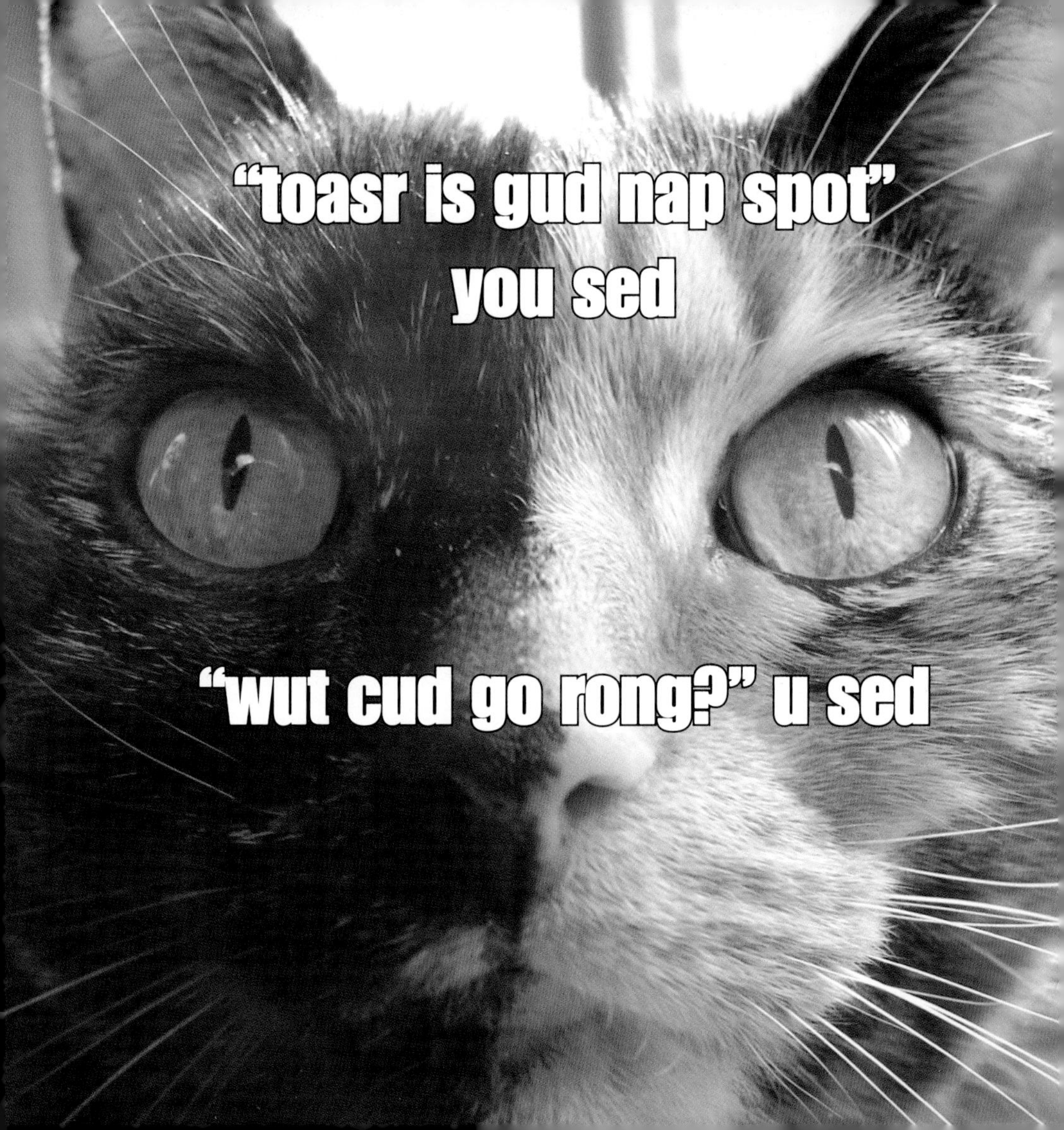
"toasr is gud nap spot"
you sed
"wut cud go rong?" u sed

**a drinking problum**

**i has it**

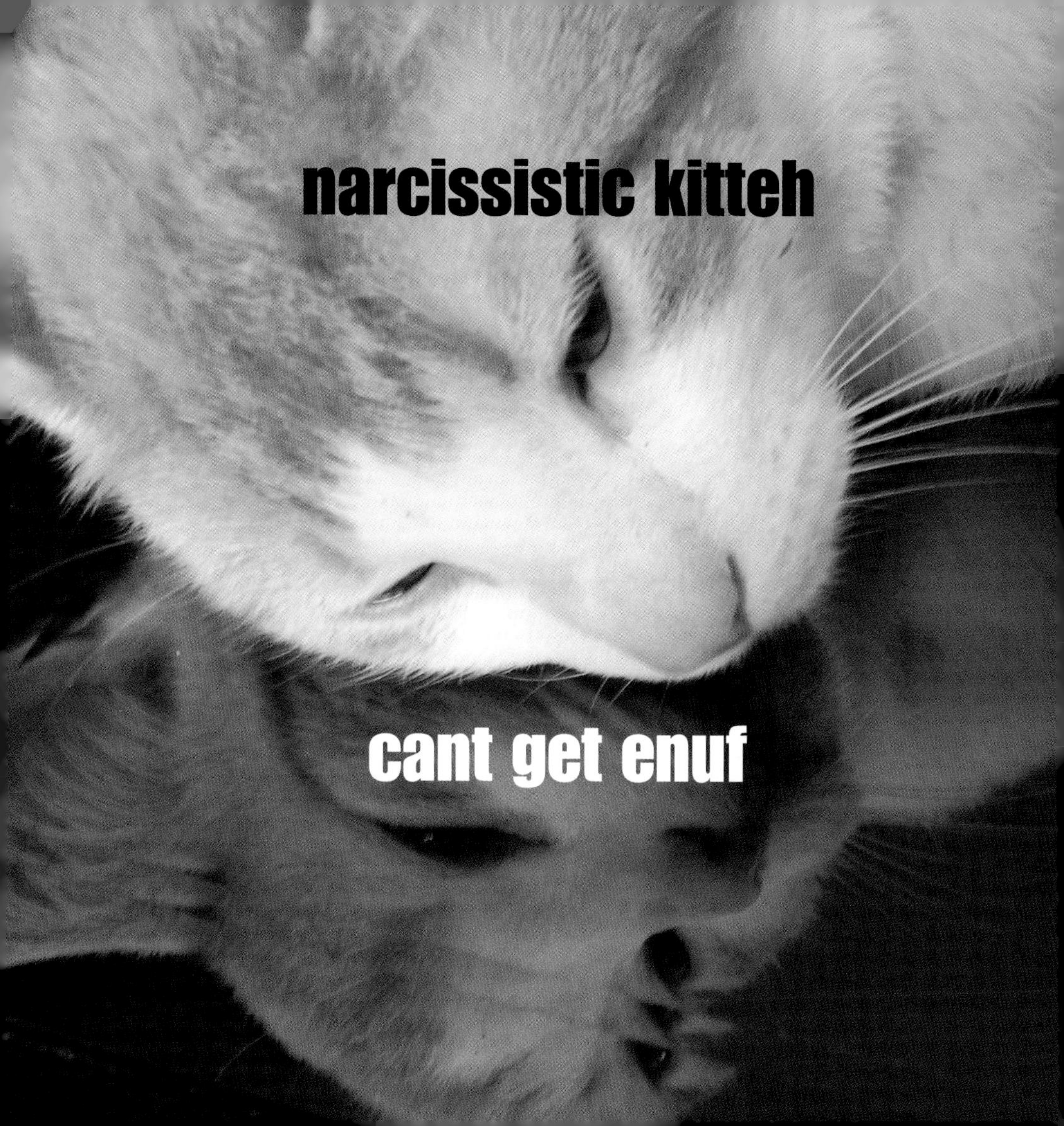
narcissistic kitteh
cant get enuf

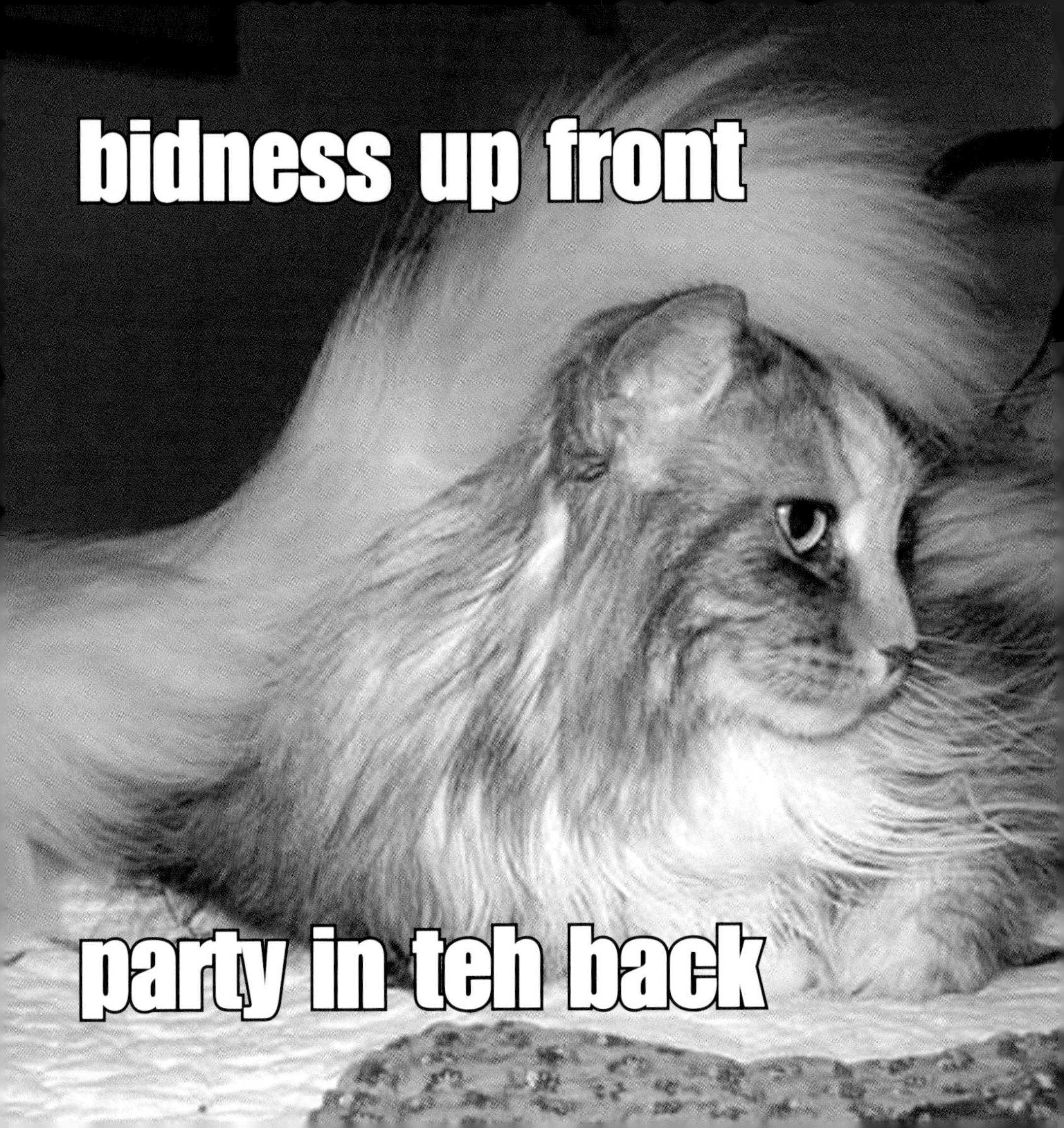
bidness up front
party in teh back

quiet cat

plots revenge

so does we has deel?

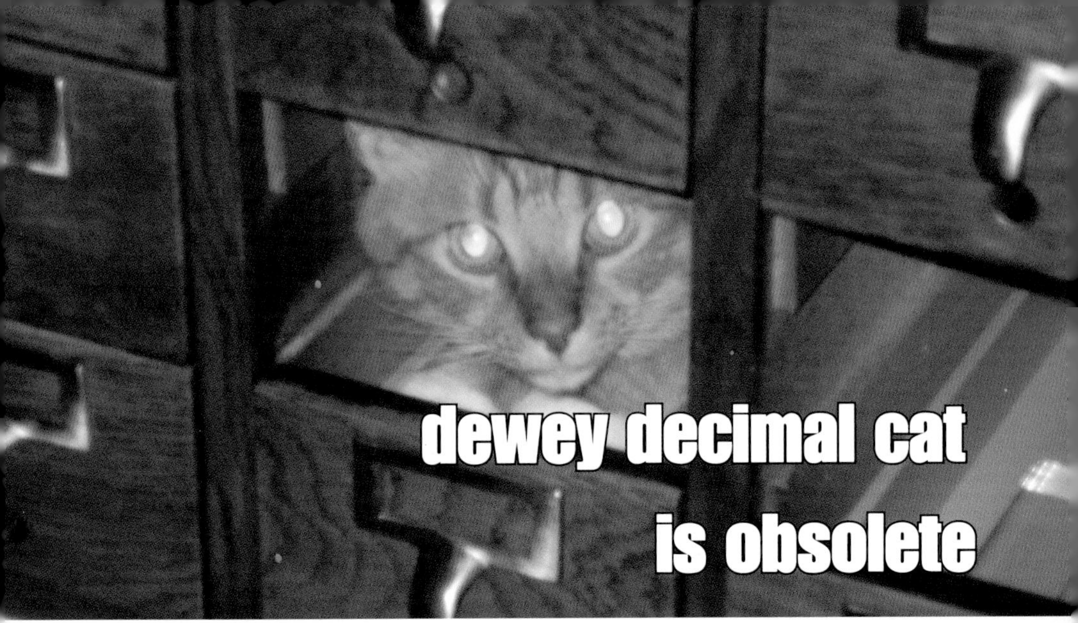
dewey decimal cat
is obsolete

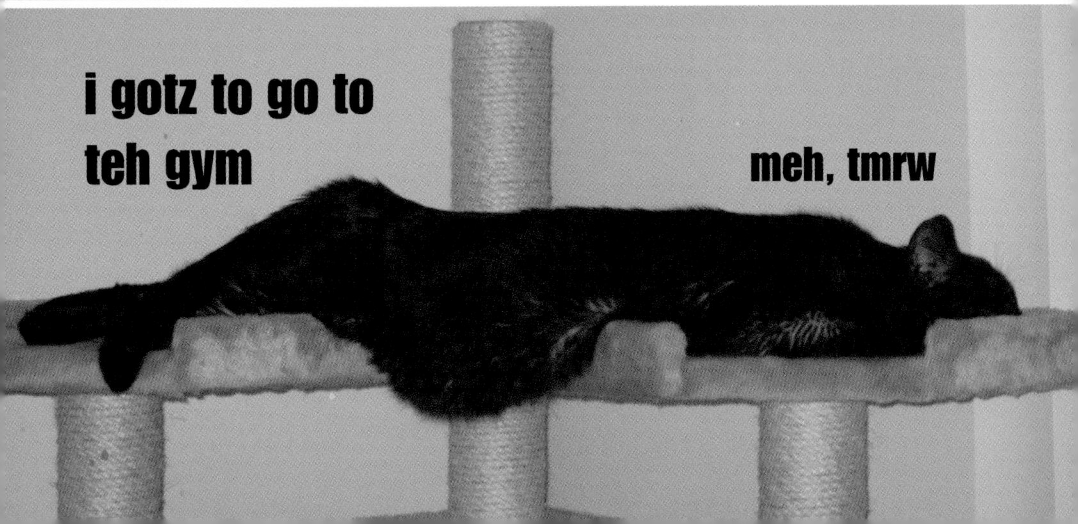
i gotz to go to
teh gym
meh, tmrw

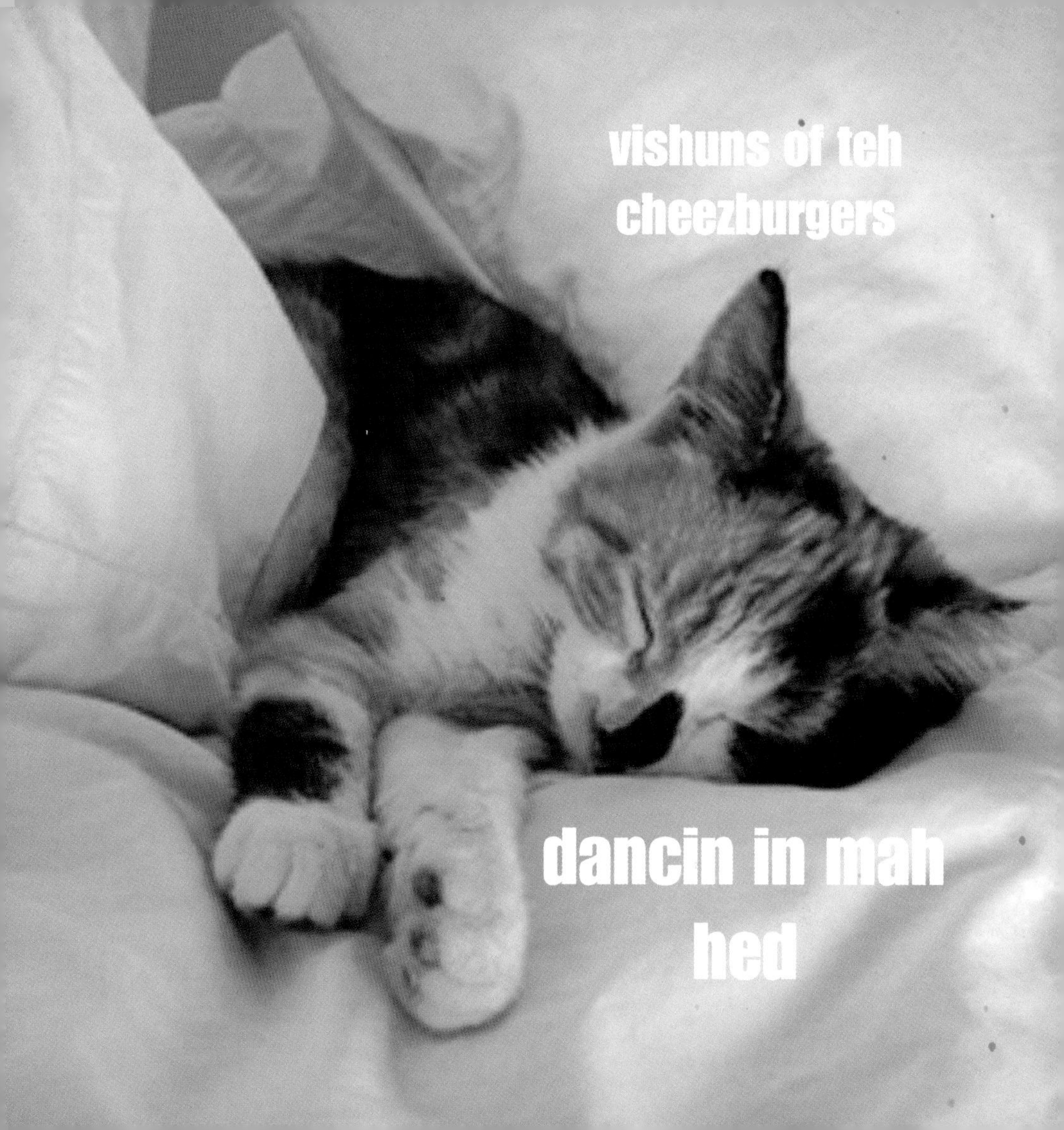
vishuns of teh cheezburgers
dancin in mah hed

i can has cheezburger to go?

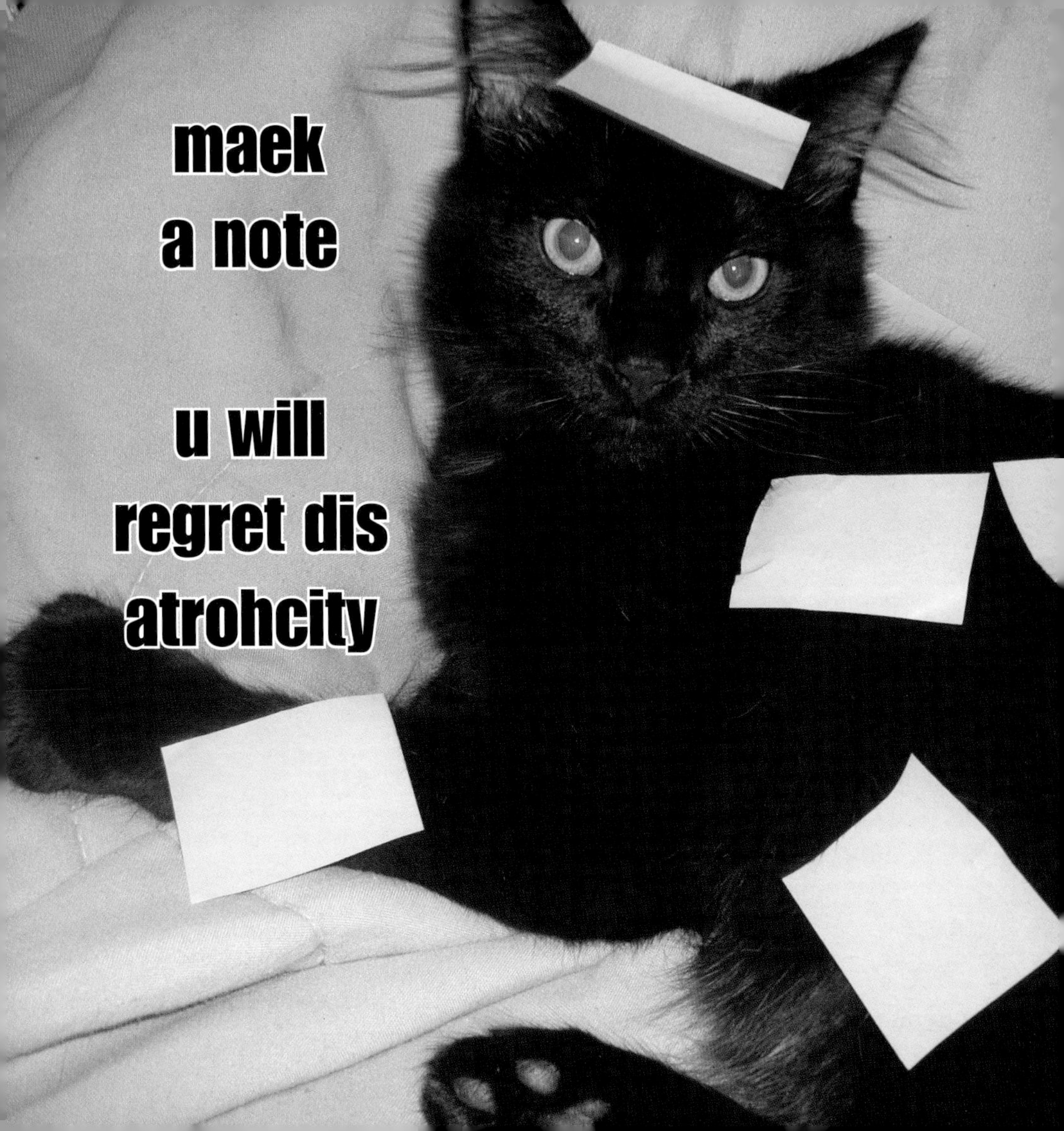
maek
a note
u will
regret dis
atrohcity

invisible
upright bass

fly
u foolz!!

I don't know
what hapn 2 ur dog

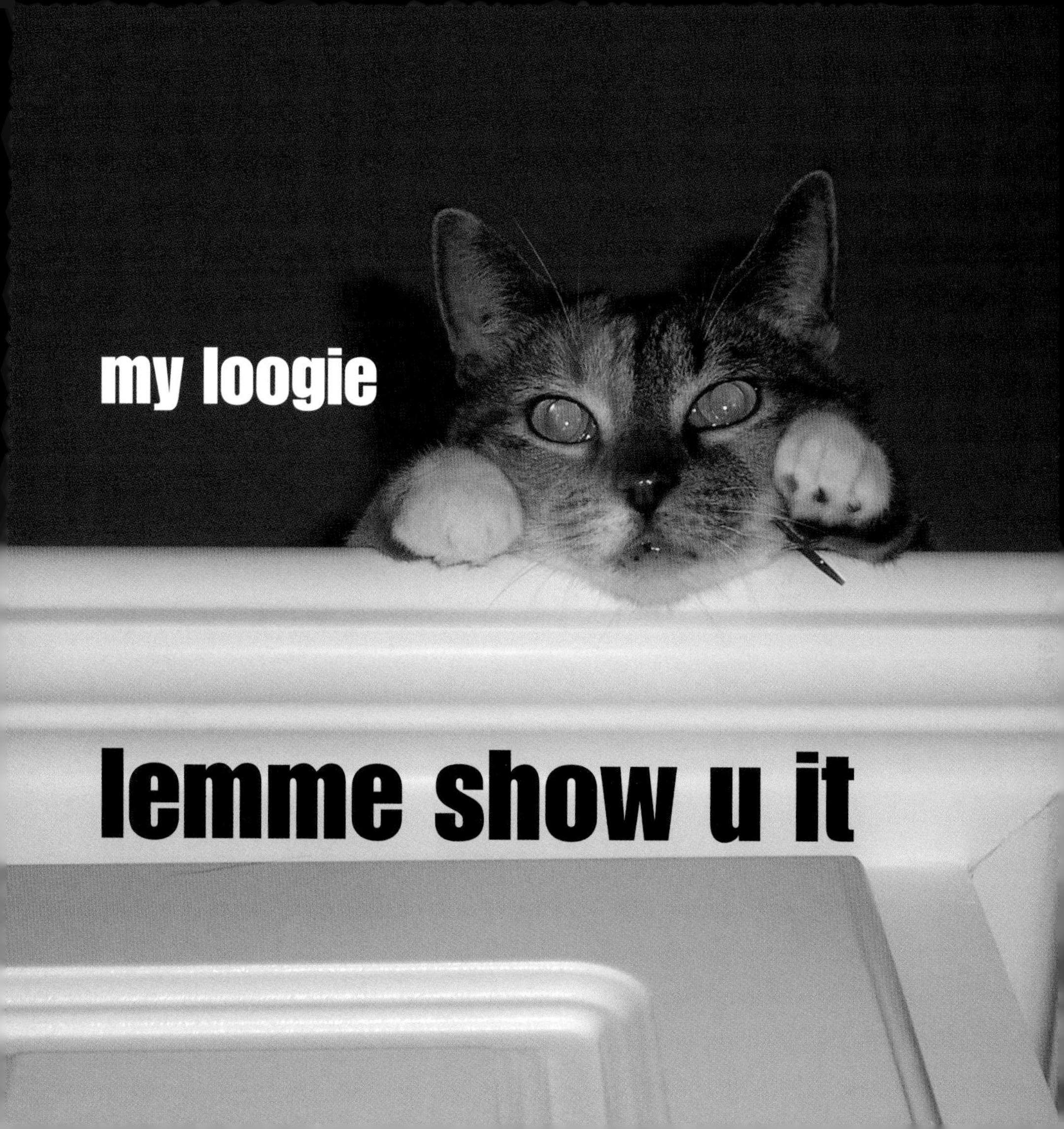
my loogie
lemme show u it

# HALP

used as an exclamashun to call fer assistance or to attract attenshun

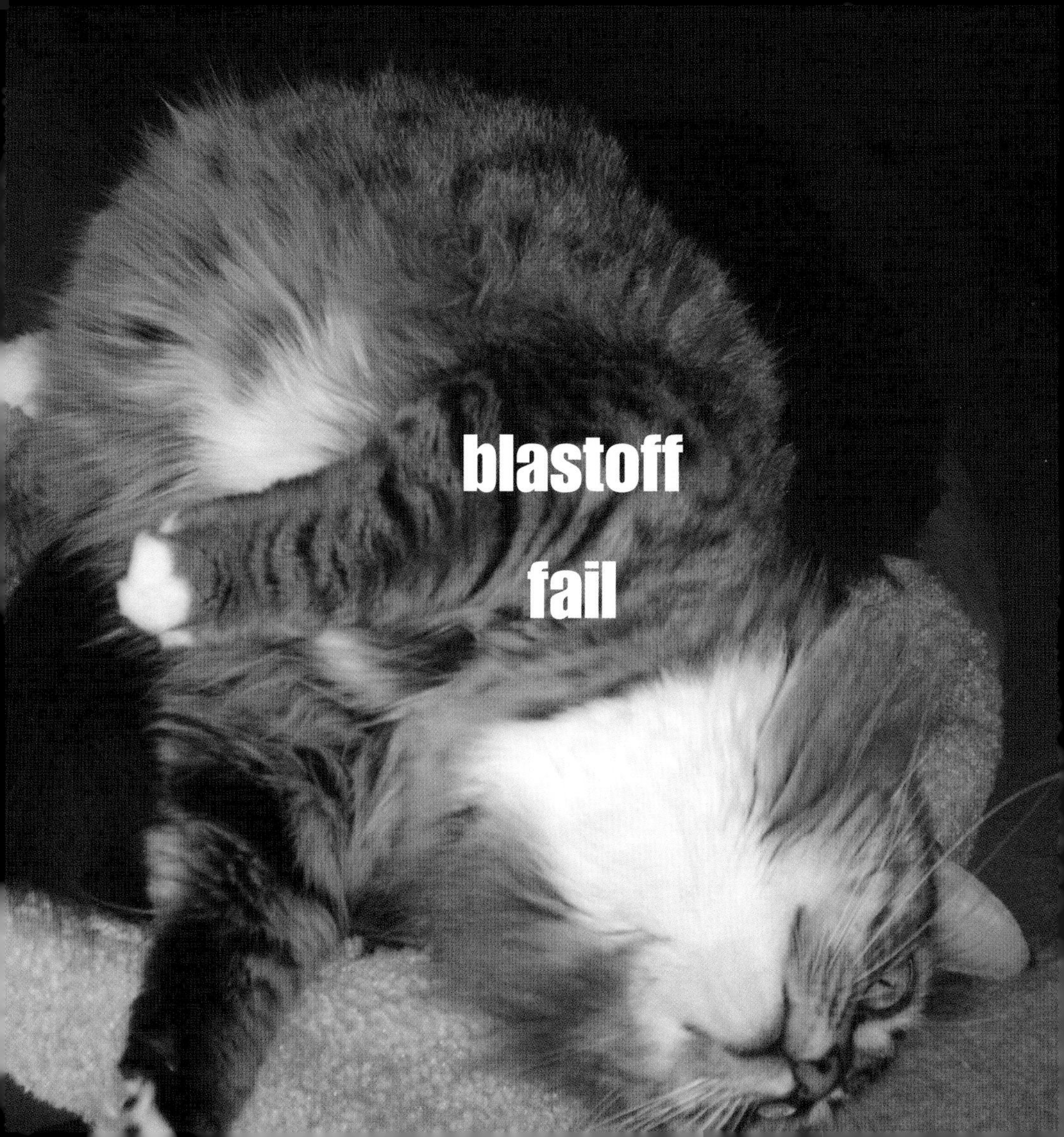
blastoff
fail

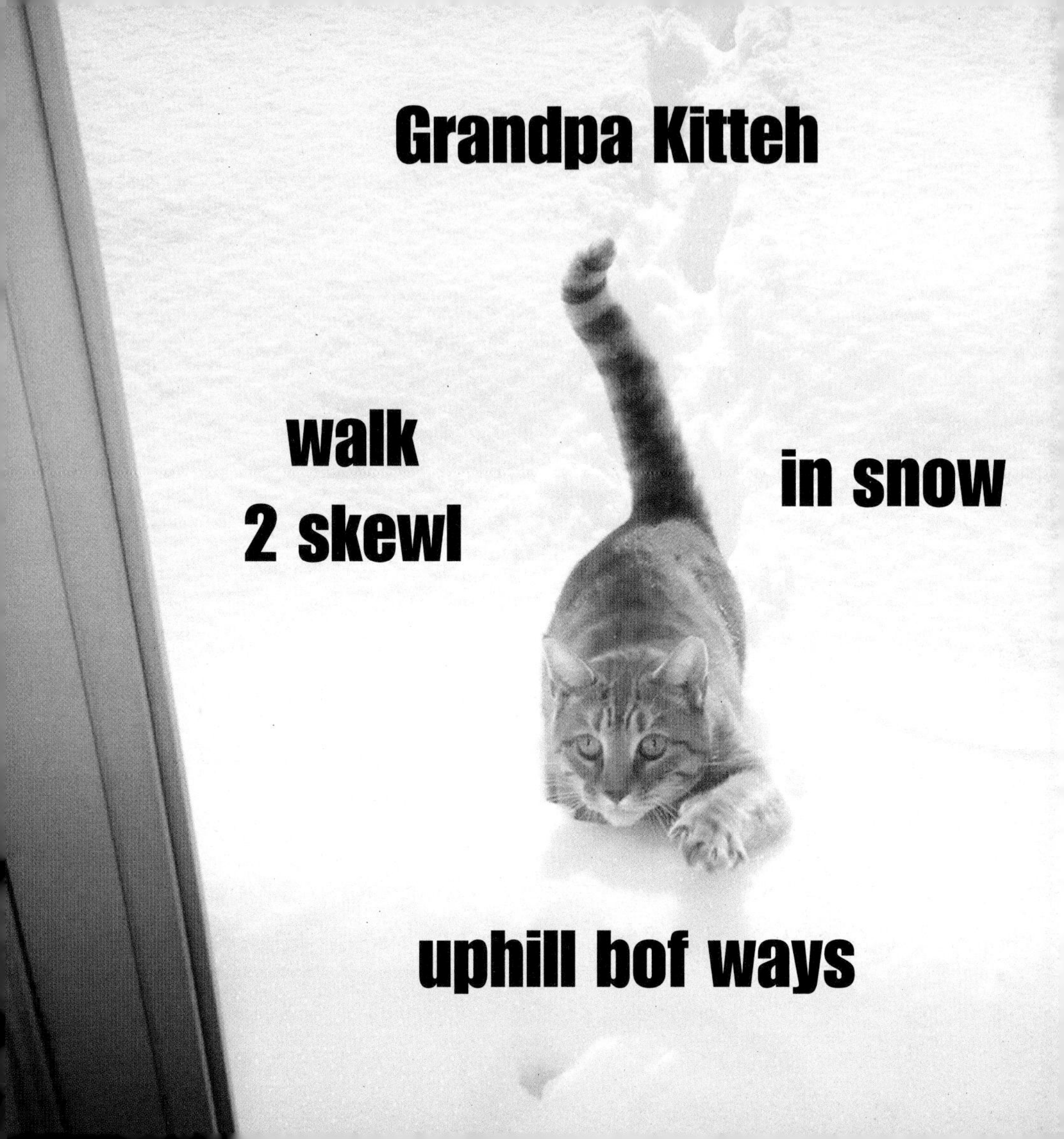
Grandpa Kitteh
walk
2 skewl
in snow
uphill bof ways

needz 5/16 shoe rench

K  let me
reech it

I HATE LOLCAT CAPTION, PLZ STOP

# Thx

We would like to thank Ben and Emily Huh and the burger team of Seattle; Kenta and Li-anne of www.otmur.com and their two kids Sammy and Pepper (see illustration) for their fun artwork and cute drawings; Citron & Deutsch, for guidance and patience; Hector Gray of Incrediballistic, for coding the cheezburger factory; MJ, the kissing ninja; Photobucket; WordPress!; Matt, for giving us a chance; Lloyd, for answering our e-mails at 4 A.M.; Barry, for fixing CSS/PHP bugs; Sam + Joseph + Gordon and the rest of the Automattic team; Anil Dash, for his poignant synopsis of what cheezburgers mean to cats; Xeni Jardin and Boing Boing for finding humor in the insane; David McRaney, for thinking hard and writing harder; Scott Beale of Laughing Squid, for always filtering his photos for the best shots; Gordon McNaughton of the original lolcat builder; Barce, the code ninja, Kitty de Medici, queen of captions, Sara Snee and the Flickr Can Has Cheezburger group, and all lolbrarians, for collecting and contributing caps; friends at Catster + Dogster; Chris + Wil at Spunge; Brunetto T-shirts; JS-Kit, the best rating engine; Gmail and 25GB expanded storage; Firefox 2 + Tab Mix Plus, for saving our lives and cluttering our minds; cat lovers around the world; and **IMPACT FONT**. Special thanks to Patrick Mulligan of Gotham for tracking down photo rights and having faith in His Ceilingness (ROR!), Ben Gibson (code name "penben") for covers and layout, and to Kate McKean and Howard Morhaim Literary Agency for understanding the way of the lolz. Finally, we'd like to send a million cheezburgers and thanks to the cats . . . for humoring us.

Kari wishes to thank her mom for her unconditional support, Mr. Fusion for powering her flux capacitor, and Tribble for being tribbly.

Eric sends thanks and love to Mom, Dad, GG, Nana, Moani + Thomas, Martin + Arissa + Kailah, Ian + Brandi, Ashleigh, Carlye, Dezlee, Shannon + Nick + Tania, Thorn + Sasha + Potter, Rick + Daneen + Tam + Pher + Co + Ricky, and永美子 と 赤ちゃん‼

| LOLcat | Thx to |
|---|---|
| octopus cat is at rest | Cotton by Conrad Baker |
| OH HAI./ I BUFFED UR FLOOR. | Spencer and Mr. Pouffy by Robin AF Olson (See more at www.coveredin-cathair.com) |
| crap | Natalie Fritz |
| I made you a cookie.../ but I eated it. | Jimmy Leo (www.flickr.com/photos/babykailan) |
| best sock evar | Kyle by Dayna Abel |
| RESCUE CAT DO RESCUEZ | Erin Bradley (aka "Miss Information" on Nerve.com) |
| levitashun./ i has it | Chloe by Marie Sweeten |
| OH HAI./ I DUN THE SUMZ, WE CAN BUYS NUTHER CHEEZBURGER | Diana Gallagher (www.nottingham-photography.com) |
| mai preshussss | Janine Roach |
| *SHUN* | Matthew Poole |
| MONORAIL CAT | from teh internets |
| Monorail cat haz mrgency airbrak | Xena by Barbara Smith |
| monorail kitteh/ on lift for repares | Amun-Ra by Christina Urban (DivineKittyCat) |
| IZ MAI OWN HAIRS/ RLY. | anonymous kitteh |
| EXPLAIN PLZ/ im confusd | Picklo by Steven Pusey |
| turn the gravity back on, ok hal? | Michael C. Berch |
| gah!!!/ is full of starz!!! | Kurt Gegenhuber of The Celestial Monochord |
| thermostat cat/ iz not maed uv mon-ies/ put on a swetter | Lazarus by Ashley Weaver |
| retrn 2 sendr | Maggie Osterberg (www.flickr.com/photos/mediawench and www.mediawench.com) |
| Needs halp?/ I canz do fotoshop | Briar-Brae Maugrim of Brenna by Barb Belanger |
| catmoflage actv8td | Janine Roach |
| AAAHHHHH See anything?? | photo by Giane Portal (www.flickr.com/photos/fofurasfelinas); caption by Leslie Klenke (www.spares-thequid.com) |
| hey/ i was watching that! | anonymous kitteh |
| I ARE SERIOUS CAT/ PLZ U STEP INTO MY OFFICE NOW | anonymous kitteh |
| Naked Guy/ reely freekin me owt | Meemoo by Louise and Ian |
| aktully Jim what we see here is | Puddi by Audrey |
| SPY CAM/ installed and functioning | Phoebe Epstein |
| im in ur hole messin wif ur hed 1 2 3 4 | Julian by Mimi Baker of Dallas, TX |
| I C DEAD PEEPS | Julian by Mimi Baker of Dallas, TX |
| OFF TO MOON/ BRB | Lula |
| | Giane Portal (www.flickr.com/pho-tos/fofurasfelinas) |
| emo cat/ sits in corner | Q. McEachern |
| oh hai been scratchin ur records/ like a dj | Mike and Jenny Lokshin |
| i hope theyll be gone when i opens mah eyes | The Karaniewsky Family |
| MYARR! | Pony Lauricella |

| LOLcat | Thx to |
|---|---|
| a hedaych/ i has it | Bean and Monkey by Nora Cosgrove-Wagar |
| banker cat denies ur loan | John Fritz |
| I beleeves.../ in ceiling cat | Pony Lauricella |
| i has a punkin flavor | Chino by Kirby and Ashley Schlyer |
| a best friend... i has it | Raymond Stone |
| COD/ cat on delivery u pay nao | Bean and Monkey by Nora Cosgrove-Wagar |
| call for halp i iz stuck for realz this time | Adam Rönnegård ("With cat gone, will there be hope for man?") |
| invisible guitar solo | Emma by Casey Gardner |
| I has a job interview | Tjasa&Spela |
| censor cat/ blocks mature content | Bean and Monkey by Nora Cosgrove-Wagar |
| nom nom nom | Traci Trapani |
| litl kiteh has litl noms | Princess Nina Ballerina by Jessie Craig |
| nom nom nom nom nom | Melanie Northerner |
| nom de plume | DJ Squeakers by Deb Houghton |
| cheezburger.../ out dere... sumwheres | Trish Skinner |
| banana fone/ ringing off teh hook | Chris Pierce |
| greedy cat wants it all | Indigo by Amber Tull |
| emo kitteh/ hates pretty things | Cat-a-Clysm by Grant McDonald |
| evikshun notice SERVED | Charles J. Scheffold |
| grudge cat iz still ignoring u | James and Jess Boyer |
| financial advisor cat disapprovs of ur banking methods | Kayla Tackett |
| HAND ME THE WRENCH! | Natalie Fritz |
| Come home/ soon plz | Raymond Stone |
| IN UR QUANTUM BOX.../ ...MAYBE | Kevin Steele; caption by Dan Lurie, geekfriendly.org |
| gps cat sez u lost. | Kiki by Elizabeth Schoenfeld |
| for a brief shining moment parrot thought he won | Eisenheim and Miggy |
| ^5 | Sam and Max by Karla Anderson |
| evr hav the feelin/ ur bein watched? | Marzipan by Adam Romig |
| lazors lockd/ on intrudr | Jeff Bowers |
| Hello from ebays!/ not wut u xpected? | Rolf Jacobson |
| couch kitteh/ awaits ur arrival | The Crowe Family and Booger the cat of Dallas, TX |
| lol/ u peed ur pants | Daniel Lackey and Jill Doornbos |
| catini shaken not stirred | Frankie by Ashlee Attebery of Arlington, TX |
| Get out!/ Iz mai private times | Noble by Lili Schmidt |
| i has a mope | Simba by Judy Parker |
| emo cat wishes u wud leave. | Hip and the Faber family (Greeting the world from the Netherlands) |
| i has a hat | Lisa Hill |
| INVISIBLE LAWNMOWER | Peter Wilson (pwils10@btinternet.com) |
| invisible superman cape | Ghost by Grace Farstad and Melissa H. |

| LOLcat | Thx to |
|--------|--------|
| invisible violin solo | "Hey Bertha! This is Olga. It pays off being weird. People will accept us for who we are... as soon as we get some masks!" |
| burrito cat/ needs moar cheez plzz | BarakKhazad |
| o rly?/ chickn hat agn? | Will Wolff-Myren (www.flickr.com/photos/willwm) |
| get out/ taking bath | Merry Spratford |
| Ugh...bachelor pads. Call me when you duz lawndry | Ashley Martineau |
| caffeine crash/ i has it | Dane Purmalis |
| tonite/ while u sleep | Camden by Jocelyn Abeldt |
| kitteh frozen/ must reboot | Indigo by Amber Tull |
| CAN I PLZ HAS 2 CHEEZBURGERS 3 PUGBURGERS 6 CHIKIN NUGITS NO WAIT MAKE IT 9 | Janine Roach |
| insert cheezburger ------> | Rupert and Ashley Bryan |
| doorcat/ saw what u did there | Mike, Heather, and Oscar in Covington, GA |
| party cat/ iz partied out | Cotton by Conrad Baker |
| hesitant cat/ hesitates | Amy Papa |
| hai there/ u be my new friend? | Marloes Kleton |
| kaat furry doorstop by IKEA designer sven fuzzybottom | Dadoopie by Shuhaida and Charles Meekings |
| cloning ur doin it wrong | Cambria |
| laser eye surgery ur doin it wrong | Furrari by Kelly George |
| Facebook/ ur doin it wrong | Jeff Youngstrom (tomecat.com/madtimes) |
| handpuppet/ ur doin it wrong | Lizz Wilson |
| k...i redy./ u may add fishes nao | Liz and Todd Burnett with the Weasley Monster |
| SOME ASSEMBLIES REQUIRED | Agnes |
| GET OFF LAPTOPZ/ AND FEEDS ME DAMMIT | Bingo by Steve McPherson |
| do want | Eugene Khudenko |
| napoleon kitteh/ iz ekspandin teh empyre | Zak by Ann Smedes |
| ANGRY KAT/ NO LIKES WHEN YOU MOCKS HIM | Miss Priss by David Holmes (thx to Citizens for Animal Protection in Houston, TX) |
| have you seen.../ my pokemans? | Mary Rose Driskel |
| faces or vase? | Beth Aslakson (www.bethtoons.com) |
| chek her out/ she says she's 3 louk moar liek 7 to me! | Courtney Ortiz-Trammell and Oskie, who were introduced to ICHC by Andrew Connolly |
| do want | Mars, Simo, Lia, and Tony Cooper |
| conjoined kittehs/ hope 2 b separated somday | Daisy and Jake by Adele Maestranzi |
| coffee iz reddee!!1! | For Sam Barton, serving our country overseas |
| no camras kthxbai | Brian & Ashley Martineau |
| great night/ I'll call you, k? | Victoria Hiley |

| LOLcat | Thx to |
|--------|--------|
| im in ur tube/ blockin ur internets | Martin Cathrae (http://flickr.com/photos/suckamc/) |
| passwurd plz?/ kthx | Andrew Todd |
| atlas cat/ can always finds u | Stephane Jeanrenaud |
| KITTEH CAN HAS/ PERSONAL SPACE?! | Megan Flaherty |
| where mah cheezburger?! | Maren Stewart |
| grab my paw if you wantz to live | Milli by Laura Poncik |
| time warp kitteh is phasing out | Idgie by Laura Cox |
| AFK | Cambria |
| i tink we haz a mowse problum... | Pony Lauricella |
| This won't end up on the internet will it? | Grey Bear by Nick and Dara |
| Nosy Neighbor cat/ sees u hidin teh bodies | Norman by Anne Tudor |
| oh here's ur problum/ dis car is a tabl | Nicole Gaddis |
| after face lift/ u do mah nose. | Kitty Lumpkins by Veronika and Douglas Elsaesser |
| dis doesn't concern u/ move along | Randy E. Winn (lawyersforwarriors.blogspot.com) |
| nite nite bunneh/ c u in teh mornin! | Stencer |
| Caturday iz great | Baboo by Amber Edwards |
| DIS A JOEK RITE? | Gracie Grohmann |
| nom nom nom nom | Carmelynn Cole |
| WAIT I WILL HELPS YOU TYEP! *** | Jade by Davezilla of Davezilla.com |
| DIS NOT RIGHT KIND/ BUT I EETED ANYWAY | Lou Piniella by Andreah Weitz (kickarsedesign@gmail.com) |
| BUFF Cat/ is overcompensating | Craig Klein |
| going somewheres? | Tiger by Lisa Jennings |
| o ur floor so much awe-sum!!!1!/ litez poken me all over | Dan Oldre |
| IM IN UR GARDEN/ SCARIN UR KIDS | Aslaug Svava Jonsdottir and Karl Gunnarsson |
| under ur van/ messin wif ur enjins | Jonas Voss |
| im in ur chair watchin ur mooveez | Jim McClear |
| im in ur dishwasher/ waitin fer my showr | Molly Kleinman |
| I cans lift/ u spot | Zippy and Noodles by Arron Coates |
| I regret to inform you that/ ii: p[[[[[[[[[[[[[[[[[[[[[[[[ | Fredrik Linge Nygaard |
| HALP!!!1!/ Space Invadrz eatin mah bwains % | Stimpy by Dan Dalmasso |
| Jus 5 moar minits.../ pleez? | Gobi by Anne Huys |
| GIT UR OWN | Courtney Ortiz-Trammell and Oskie, who were introduced to ICHC by Andrew Connolly |
| NEED MOAR HOTPOCKETS! | Emma Kowal |
| NO | Breakfast by Michael and Rhonda Smith |
| Solar powered Kitteh/ iz recharging | Mike Blanche |
| TEH CRINKLY NOIZE/ ITZ FANTASTIC!!1 | B.B. by Holly and Andy |
| nooo, Randy, don't doo it!!! | Fredrik Linge Nygaard |
| new happy meal toyz/ iz been in there for dayz | Nathan and Mary Rowan |

| LOLcat | Thx to |
|---|---|
| papr covers rock | Django and Bailey by Lisa Wohl |
| polygraph kitteh/ detects deception | Dana Couture, Sue Masel, and Scooter |
| SIDE EFFECTS INCLUDE:/ MOOD SWINGS LOSS OF APPETITE HAIR LOSS | Jasmine by Rox Church |
| raised by armadillos | Brett Guillory |
| NO!1!/ no mor relity tv!1!! | Julie Parker-Garza, Juanita Haggard, and Staci Haggard <3 Teddy! |
| QWIK!! get mom nao!1!!!/ itz crushin meeee!!1!! | Tiger by Stacy Davidson |
| relaxashun yu doin it rite | Sable by Eric and Marie Sproul |
| LAZER SETTINGS:/ KILL STUN MAIM | Robin "Violist" Leung |
| sleep.../...i needz it | Bart Klein Reesink |
| smug kitteh/ iz pleased wit own acheevments | Bindi by Katie Graham |
| ceiling cat iz watching u | From teh internets |
| Thank u, ceiling cat/ 4 catnip n Caturday | Daniela |
| Oh, hai ceiling cat./ U scare me. | Gatti by Christina Decurtis |
| i has a flavr | Mars, Simo, Lia, and Tony Cooper |
| i darez yu to kross/ no i daroz yu to kross | Pony Lauricella |
| Those who can't do.../ nap. | Bob Cat Rob Bob by Emma-Leigh Johnson |
| you godda roll wiv it | Raynah Thomas |
| Iz stuck. Bring hunny. | Women, Fire & Dangerous Things (http://flickr.com/photos/wfdt/) |
| TIS STUF IZ GUDD | Prince by Shawnee Altman |
| To get prey.../ ...must be liek prey | David and Kathleen Thomas |
| "toasr is gud nap spot" you sed./ "wut cud go rong?" u sed. | Craig Elliot (www.flickr.com/photos/tjflex/301347804/) |
| WANT | Jacqueline Collar (chey-sama.deviantart.com) |
| a drinking problum/ i has it | Mad Max |
| narcissistic kitteh/ cant get enuf | Angela Buchanan |
| bidness up front/ party in teh back | Carmelynn Cole |
| quiet cat/ plots revenge | Candice Frey |
| so does we has deel? | Candice Frey |
| may i drive/ use ur blinker!!1! | Porter by Rhonda Hobson |
| dewey decimal cat is obsolete | Sarah and Robert Ferguson |
| i gotz to go to teh gim/ meh, tmrw | Loki the Fat (may you live large and prosper) |
| vishuns of teh cheezburgers/ dancin in mah hed | Ben Gibson |
| i haz fort/ no tell girlz | Moe by Ryan Keighley |
| i can has cheezburger to go? | Jackie Fritsche of Eatontown, NJ (www.flickr.com/photos/sis) |
| maek a note/ u will regret dis atrohcity | Katie Holt |
| i is ur toy/ try me! | Skye Driggs |
| invisible upright bass | Daniela |
| fly u foolz!! | Daniela |
| getitoff! getitoff! | Daniela |
| i don't know what hapn 2 ur dog | Cyb3rD0n Architectus |
| ur presentz?/ I ate em | Dylan by Erin Fox and Benjamin Stansfield |
| invisible kick 2 teh gut | Norman by Holly and Andy |
| im on ur table/ performin mitosis | Smeagol & Zombie by Holly and Andy |
| my loogie/ lemme show u it | Bonez by Holly and Andy |
| refleckshun cat iz spoooky | Ben Gibson |
| iz 4 u | Mitsu by Lucinda Laveck |
| halp! it eating meh!! | Benny by Sarah Rogers |
| LITTLE HALP/ kthx! | Thanks to Lifelong Friends in Lago Vista, TX for saving Marlow - Amy Casdorph |
| HALP/ Mah graviteez iz broked!!1! | Sarah Wilbur |
| i haz a pillo/ i haz a blanket | Utzu Garcés |
| blastoff fail | Candice Frey |
| Grandpa Kitteh/ walk 2 skewl in snow/ uphill bof ways | Gilbert by Jane Tilton |
| Needz 5/16 shoe-rench/ K let me reech it | Cali and Khmer by Catherine Y. Bae |
| I HATE LOLCAT CAPTION. PLZ STOP | Rudy by Michele Ferrario (http://www.mferrario.it/latente) |